Rising Consumer Materialism

Rising Consumer Materialism presents a theoretical advancement of materialism research. It identifies eight inter-disciplinary areas of a consumer's life of prime importance to the promotion of a happy and rewarding lifestyle. This study examines the pre-planned purchase process as the primary step towards satisfactory consumption. The theoretical framework provides a stream of research possibilities that guide readers towards healthy consumption patterns. Therefore, the book offers practical solutions to problems such as loneliness and unhappiness. It advocates a new dimension of consumption activity and lifestyle choices that can help in re-socialization and the improvement of social bonds – hitting materialism right at its core, while making the consumption experience well-informed and beneficial for the consumer as well as society.

Together, pre-planned engagement, intrinsic experiential purchases with a view to environmentalism, religiosity, social giving, social support and nostalgia can cure the excessive emphasis on acquiring and showing off valuables that is disruptive to a consumer's social affiliations and subjective well-being.

Since the consumer's use of material possessions as a proxy measure for success and happiness results in only temporary happiness, discontent, continuous brand/product switching, undesirable post-purchase evaluations and shifting brand loyalties, the book establishes alternative mechanisms for achieving happiness. The integrated framework provides a comprehensive solution rather than a half-baked specific situation-based interventions, and the book is a must read for academics, students and consumers alike.

Afia Khalid is a PhD Scholar at the National College of Business Administration & Economics, Lahore, Pakistan.

Faisal Qadeer is an Associate Professor and the Head of the Research Programme at Lahore Business School, University of Lahore, Pakistan.

Routledge Focus on Business and Management

The fields of business and management have grown exponentially as areas of research and education. This growth presents challenges for readers trying to keep up with the latest important insights. Routledge Focus on Business and Management presents small books on big topics and how they intersect with the world of business.

Individually, each title in the series provides coverage of a key academic topic, whilst collectively, the series forms a comprehensive collection across the business disciplines.

ISSN: 2475–6369

For a complete list of titles in this series, please visit www.routledge.com/business/series/FBM

Rising Consumer Materialism

A Threat to Sustainable Happiness

Afia Khalid and Faisal Qadeer

Routledge
Taylor & Francis Group

LONDON AND NEW YORK

First published 2018
by Routledge
2 Park Square, Milton Park, Abingdon, Oxon OX14 4RN

and by Routledge
605 Third Avenue, New York, NY 10017

First issued in paperback 2021

Routledge is an imprint of the Taylor & Francis Group, an informa business

Publisher's Note
The publisher has gone to great lengths to ensure the quality of this reprint but points out that some imperfections in the original copies may be apparent.

British Library Cataloguing-in-Publication Data
A catalogue record for this book is available from the British Library

Library of Congress Cataloging-in-Publication Data
Names: Khalid, Afia, 1984- author. | Qadeer, Faisal, 1969- author.
Title: Rising consumer materialism : a threat to sustainable happiness / Afia Khalid and Faisal Qadeer.
Description: Abingdon, Oxon ; New York, NY : Routledge, 2018. | Includes bibliographical references and index.
Identifiers: LCCN 2017040786 (print) | LCCN 2017050742 (ebook) | ISBN 9781351256926 (eBook) | ISBN 9780815367598 (hardback : alk. paper)
Subjects: LCSH: Consumers. | Consumer behavior. | Consumption (Economics)—Social aspects. | Materialism.
Classification: LCC HC79.C6 (ebook) | LCC HC79.C6 K4195 2018 (print) | DDC 306.3—dc23
LC record available at https://lccn.loc.gov/2017040786

ISBN 13: 978-1-03-209612-4 (pbk)
ISBN 13: 978-0-8153-6759-8 (hbk)

Typeset in Times New Roman
by Swales & Willis Ltd, Exeter, Devon, UK

Contents

Figures

Tables

Preface

Today's global world is marked by rising consumerism and brand absorption. This has resulted in several consumer issues, such as incoherent lifestyles, depression, anxiety, loneliness, sadness and so on. Amongst these the most distressing is the rising level of materialism. Materialism is insatiable attachment to worldly possessions and is believed to be making consumers selfish, egoistic and non-social. It therefore has a detrimental effect on social relationships, rendering consumers lonely, dissatisfied and unhappy. The problem with materialism starts when material possessions are utilized as a proxy measure for success or happiness, rather than for their utility. The consumer alienates themselves in the process and as a result becomes trapped in an unending cyclical loneliness and unhappiness. Subsequently, the lack of happiness leads to continuous brand/product switching, undesirable post-purchase evaluations and shifting brand loyalties, which is a concern for both theorists and marketers alike.

Therefore, it is increasingly becoming imperative to advance the theoretical knowledge on materialism and craft a cohesive, multi-disciplinary materialism theory that provides a practical solution to problems such as loneliness and unhappiness. This book provides the first comprehensive and integrated solution to the call for a method of leaving the materialism trap, using prior knowledge from different disciplines. It attempts to identify the role of materialism and its sub facets in relation to consumer happiness and the conscious breaking free from the trap, and to discover the contingencies that can modify the cycle. It also advocates a new dimension of consumption activities that can help to re-socialize the consumer and improve social bonds, hitting materialism right at its root, making the consumption experience well-informed and beneficial for the consumer as well as society.

To allow the reader to understand the depth of the existing literature on materialism, a systematic review of the major theoretical contributions was undertaken, which identified gaps in the literature giving rise to research questions and subsequent propositions. The theory-building process identified the

major and contingency constructs. The theory identifies that conscious intervention in consumption patterns, both social and psychological, provides a
framework that ensures greater satisfaction from the purchase experience,
wider social good, environmental sustainability, continued brand loyalty
and sustained happiness. It also provides a cohesive dimension of consumption that opens up a whole new agenda for future research, both theoretical
and practical. This book discusses the foundation and theoretical groundings
of the Socio-Psychological Theory of the Materialism-Loneliness-Happiness Trap and the impact of each contingency factor, along with the theory's
limitations and prospective directions.

Acknowledgements

My first and foremost obligation is to Allah Almighty, for His benevolence and countless blessings which gave me the fervour to initiate, continue and complete my work.

Then I wish to acknowledge the support and contributions of a number of people who were instrumental in the completion of this book.

Most importantly I am obliged to my mentor Dr Faisal Qadeer for his endless help, patience and insight and his remarkable expertise. I owe him each word of my work as his emotional and enlightened support, encouragement and work ethic always prompted me towards my goal and have been of immense significance in the completion of my work. His kind help and guidance was readily available at every moment throughout the process of comprehending and writing. It was his leadership and guidance that kept me steadfast to my work and eventually made it possible.

Special thanks to my mother Farhat Khalid who took care of my child while I contemplated and wrote this book and to my husband Wajahat Naseem for all his care and support during the whole process. My heartfelt appreciation goes to all – family members and supporters – who helped in shaping and furthering my work.

1   Introduction

1.1 Why materialism research is important

The discipline of consumer behaviour can play an important role in improving the lives of consumers. It studies the dynamic processes involved in making decisions about consumption experiences and how they affect the lives, feelings and coping capabilities of the several people involved in the process, thereby contributing to the formation of broader social marketplace realities and contextualizing marketing strategies.

The field of consumer behaviour emphasizes specifically the understanding of the underlying mechanisms that shape the pre-purchase, purchase and post-purchase decision-making processes of the consumer. One of the most important aspects of consumer culture is the core values that shape and influence the motivations, perceptions and attitude formation of consumers. The value set of the consumer greatly affects consumption choices, and understanding these underlying values and their impacts on consumer behaviour has important ramifications both theoretically and practically. One of the core values of the consumer's value set is materialism. Materialism is the importance that consumers attach to prized possessions, as they continuously strive for more, theming their lives around acquiring and possessing such valuables.

All over the world societies are experiencing a higher level of consumerism and brand absorption. The disruptive effects of consumerism and the incoherent lifestyles of consumers due to rising materialism have become a growing concern for socio-psychologists. Materialism is believed to make consumers selfish, greedy, egoistic and non-social. The significance that materialists assign to acquiring material goods takes central stage in life; it has a detrimental effect on their social relationships, damages the quality of connectedness and decreases the ability to fulfil the social needs of connectivity and intimacy. It is inversely related to psychological and subjective well-being. Consequently, even with high levels of ownership, consumers report being unhappier and lonelier than ever before. Therefore, it is increasingly becoming imperative to advance the theoretical knowledge of materialism and to craft a materialism theory for consumer happiness that is applicable to and that provides a practical solution to problems such as loneliness, dissatisfaction and unhappiness.

Materialism makes the consumer indulge in consumption patterns such that social and intimate relationships are left behind, crowded out by material valuables. When the consumer eventually perceives loneliness, which is a perception that social needs are not being met, they indulge in more consumption, as a coping mechanism, to do away with the loneliness. The consumer is thus trapped in a cycle where the lonelier they feel the more stress, marginality, anxiety and sadness they feel, the more they indulge in materialism as a coping strategy, and the lonelier they become due to the crowding-out effect of materialism. This materialism-loneliness trap becomes visible and vicious when the consumer utilizes material possessions as a proxy measure for success or happiness. In effect, the consumer is only temporarily happy and remains feeling lonely. Greater loneliness decreases the prospects for social sharing, which reduces the happiness acquired from material goods. The consumer substitutes goods for happiness but soon realizes the emptiness and becomes unhappier due to lack of emotional support or loneliness. Moreover, the materialistic values are in opposition to group values, emphasizing individualism rather than collective welfare. As a result of high levels of materialism, the consumer is trapped in unending loneliness and unhappiness. The lack of happiness results in continuous brand/product switching, undesirable post-purchase evaluations and shifting brand loyalties, which is a concern for both theorists and marketers alike.

The earlier consumer research has focused either upon understanding the impacts of materialism from the standpoint of different disciplines or called for ways to 'dematerialize' lifestyle. A recent wave has also talked about new materialism, whereby materialistic lifestyles should be accepted and not criticized, the only requirement being the control of materialistic pursuits beyond a certain level. This new materialism has gained momentum in recent years but provides a limited solution. Nonetheless, materialistic values are dominant enough to make dematerialization an impractical solution and simply understanding the sociological, cultural, economic and psychological impacts of materialism remains only a half-baked theoretical contribution. The inability to provide a comprehensive interdisciplinary theory for regulating materialism has kept it unleashed, which is troublesome to cope with. In both theories there is a lack of cohesiveness around dealing with materialism in a balanced way that is not disruptive for the consumer. Therefore, this study is the first to answer the call for a method for leaving the materialism trap in a cohesive manner that inculcates prior knowledge from different disciplines. It also advocates a new dimension of consciously altering consumption-process activities and engaging in socio-cultural activities that can help in re-socialization and the improvement of social bonds – hitting materialism right at its root.

Since no concrete theoretical efforts have been made to provide an understanding of the contingencies in which the consumer can break free from the Materialism-Loneliness-Happiness (MLH) trap, the existing research remains inadequate in making the phenomenon directly researchable. Furthermore, there is little understanding of the role of the three facets of materialism in relation to consumer happiness. This book focuses on iden-tifying the role of materialism and its sub facets in relation to consumer happiness by enabling a conscious breaking free of the materialism-loneliness-happiness trap, as well as uncovering contingencies that can farther mitigate the cycle.

To assist the reader in understanding the depth of the existing literature on materialism, a systematic review of the major theoretical contributions is carried out, identifying the major themes, on the basis of which four general questions are elaborated:

a) Can materialism be regarded as a negative consumer value only?
b) Can changes in the sub facets of materialism lead to a greater and continued level of happiness?
c) What are the contingencies to the way consumers behave that can miti-gate the materialism-loneliness trap?
d) What are the factors that can lessen the impact of loneliness on con-sumer happiness?

In essence these questions help to explain the theoretical understanding of materialism and related constructs. The contriving of a multidisciplinary framework for curbing materialism and mitigating its negative impacts is important both for the advancement of the study of consumer behaviour (as a discipline and as case studies) and so that the materialism theory can be applied towards consumer happiness. The proposed Socio-Psychological Theory of the Materialism-Loneliness-Happiness Trap is intended to make the consumption experience well informed and beneficial for the consumer as well as society. Conscious intervention into consumption patterns, social-giving patterns, cultural patterns and nostalgic orientations provides a theoretical and practical framework that ensures greater satisfaction with the purchase experience; improved social goodness, environmental care and sustainability; continued brand loyalties; and sustained happiness. It also provides a cohesive dimension of consumption that opens up a whole new agenda for future research.

1.2 Significance of materialism trap research for academia

The book attempts for the first time to investigate and theorize the materialism and loneliness trap and its impact on consumer happiness. It will not only provide a systematic review of the materialism literature, but will also subsequently introduce a comprehensive framework in the form of the Socio-Psychological Theory of the MLH Trap, encompassing consumption patterns and other factors that will supplement materialism research. The framework will advance academic understanding of the phenomena involved by providing a cross-over underpinning for the combined psychological, cultural and social factors surrounding the consumer. Moreover, the study will also provide theoretical foundations that will steer marketing practitioners towards using advertising appeals that modify and promote happier consumption patterns.

Consumers often exhibit post-purchase discontent and unhappiness with the purchases they make, resulting in continuous product and brand switching. The proposed theory may help practitioners to train consumers to adopt certain consumption patterns that make them happy with their purchases and promote loyalty. Moreover, the study identifies two areas of promotional appeal that can be used in advertising and promotions that increase not only the chances of higher sales but also of happier consumers.

The field of consumer behaviour revolves around understanding the various facets of the consumption process, the socio-psychological setup of the consumer and the ways in which buying behaviour could be made more informed and effective. Marketing campaigns usually stem from this understanding and are aimed at making consumers happier, and satisfied with their consumption, such that they remain a constant source of brand equity. However, each year a higher number of consumers report dissatisfaction and unhappiness with their purchases and often switch brands without apparent product/service failure. Therefore, despite decades of marketing campaign design, the delight and happiness promised for the consumer is ultimately unachieved and remains fragmented. The paradox is that even with ever-increasing budgets for advertising, brand management, marketing and amassing trade volumes, consumer happiness is reportedly plummeting.

This book focuses on the fact that marketing campaigns and various attempts to promote consumer happiness are often misdirected. Such efforts usually push the consumer towards greater materialism, loneliness and distress rather than bringing happiness. A happier consumer will be ethically embedded and more loyal, making the sustainability of happiness an important determinant of individual, social and marketing effectiveness. Nonetheless, it seems difficult to achieve such sustainability, as the solutions provided by several happiness studies are only half-baked and do not present comprehensive, sustainable solutions, due to ineffective identification of the obstacles.

The book, however, identifies that a major hindrance to sustainable consumer happiness is being ensnared in the materialism-loneliness-happiness trap and that sustainable happiness can be only achieved by untangling the trap through the contingencies identified by the Socio-Psychological Theory of the MLH Trap, as developed and explained in this book. The theory posits that the trap becomes vicious when the consumer utilizes material possessions as a proxy measure for success or happiness and attempts to buy happiness with money. In the process the consumer becomes socially disruptive. Moreover, the attempt usually fails due to the lack of social sharing prospects, resulting in greater loneliness. The void created by the lack of happiness results in continuous brand/product switching, undesirable post-purchase evaluations and shifting brand loyalties. The book attempts to develop and explain the Socio-Psychological Theory of the MLH Trap as a generalized theory for sustainable consumer happiness. Hence, it can contribute to sustainable consumer happiness and effective marketing campaigns and advertising aimed at consumer happiness such that the true purposes of marketing campaigns and consumer behaviour studies are attained.

1.3 Introduction to the main concepts

Materialism

Materialism is considered an accumulation of certain personality traits that differentiate a materialist from a non-materialist, such as greed, resentment, self-centredness and lack of generosity (Belk, 1984). Materialism is a 'craving for worldly possessions' as a steering value of life that ensures happiness and success in a materialist's belief (Richins and Dawson, 1992). There are three aspects of materialism, namely: *centrality* (major goal in life is acquiring worldly possessions), *happiness* (quest for material goods is the primary source of satisfaction) and *success* (worldly possessions act as an indicator of success to others) (Richins and Dawson, 1992).

Loneliness

Loneliness is a relatively persistent experience of emotional suffering caused by rejection or exclusion by others from a social group, being misunderstood and alienated, lacking suitable and desirable social partners for various activities, specifically the events that furnish prospects for intimacy and a sense of communal integration (Rook, 1984). It occurs when there is a perception that the quantity, significance and quality of social relationships do not meet the social needs of an individual (Gordon, 1976).

Happiness

Happiness is a measure of psychological and subjective well-being. It is a state of mind that results from being eudemonically and hedonically satisfied (Fave et al., 2011). It is an amalgam of factors including personality traits such as self-esteem, extraversion, optimism and self-control, the time frame in which happiness is being measured, and the life role being played at any point of time. It is composed of three related mechanisms which are: positive affect, absence of negative affect and satisfaction with life as a whole (Lu, 1999).

The relationship between these three constructs gives rise to the materialism-loneliness-happiness trap. This trap develops eventually due to the intensification of a materialistic lifestyle that triggers high levels of loneliness and a resulting low level of happiness. Consumers, highly engaged in materialistic pursuits, substitute material possessions for people. They become self-centred and power centric, exhibit lower intrinsic satisfaction and show lower ethical consideration. Such consumers usually develop strong group ties with other high materialists. So the whole group becomes deficient in out-group socialization capabilities. These habitual patterns shape their social circumstances in such a way as to cause them to feel lonely. Other impacts of materialism (discussed later) make such consumers depressive and discontent. The more they try to gain happiness, the tighter the knot becomes.

1.4 What this book will achieve

This book establishes a unified theory of sustained happiness for lonely materialistic consumers, a theory called the Socio-Psychological Theory of the MLH Trap. It provides a theoretical framework for materialism principles that revolves around a consumer's life from different standpoints and gives a baseline that can help in evaluating and understanding materialism from both the micro and macro aspects, at individual level and later at group and societal level. It also takes into account the different aspects of the consumption process and the motivations behind it. Little research has focused on the consumer decision-making process in totality as a complete purchase mechanism that the consumer applies at different stages of consumption, or on how the consumer exhibits materialism. The study can effectively contribute towards the understanding of the decision-making process at a finer level. Furthermore it effectively establishes that materialism can be curbed and manipulated through changes in consumption behaviour.

The conceptual clarity of materialism and related processes set out in the book will enable consumers to effectively enlarge their consumption experience and enjoy a higher level of satisfaction with their purchase and experiences. Moreover it will help consumers to relish a sustained level of happiness as better consumers, users and givers within society. Marketers can effectively reduce the level of product dissatisfaction and brand switching by educating the consumer about evaluation-process potholes. Moreover it may help marketers to streamline their advertising appeals according to the experiential and nostalgic aspects of their products and services.

The Socio-Psychological Theory of the Materialism-Loneliness-Happiness Trap makes a significant theoretical contribution through the investigation and theorization of the materialism-loneliness trap and its impact on consumer happiness. The systematic review of the materialism literature provides a theoretical framework of consumption patterns and subsequent consumer behaviour that will not only supplement materialism research but can act as a guide for happier lifestyles. It provides a cross-over underpinning of the combined psychological, personal and social factors surrounding the consumer. Moreover, the book provides theoretical foundations steering marketing practitioners towards using advertising appeals that promote happier consumption patterns. Just as the international media has seen a shift towards advertising relying more on corporate social responsibility, there may also perhaps be a shift towards 'happier consumer'-focused advertising, with the guidance of this book. The book may also help practitioners to train consumers to adopt certain consumption patterns that make them satisfied with whatever purchases they make, irrespective of the monetary value of the purchase, and thereby promote loyalty towards the brand and satisfaction with self. Two areas of promotional appeal are identified which can be used in advertising and promotions, which not only increase the chances of higher sales but also promote happier consumers.

In a nutshell, this book can be taken as a guide for consumers, companies, brands and media campaign designers who wish for satisfying consumption experiences for both consumers and producers. The true joy, delight and satisfaction of consumption and a satisfying lifestyle is often eclipsed by materialistic pursuits and values. This overshadowing frequently drags the consumer into loneliness and other social ills. This book focuses on and highlights the fact that the solution to social ills is not that far away; rather, it lies with the consumer to a great extent and also with the media campaigners and advertisers that create the surrounding environment.

References

Belk, R. W. (1984). Three scales to measure constructs related to materialism: Reliability, validity and relationships to measures of happiness. *Advances in Consumer Research*, 11(1), 291–297.

Fave, D. A., Brdar, I., Freire, T., Vella, B. D., and Wissing, M. P. (2011). The eudaimonic and hedonic components of happiness: Qualitative and quantitative findings. *Social Indicators Research*, 100(2), 185–207.

Gordon, S. (1976). *Lonely in America*. New York, NY: Simon and Schuster.

Lu, L. (1999). Personal or environmental causes of happiness: A longitudinal analysis. *Journal of Social Psychology*, 139(1), 79–90.

Richins, M. L., and Dawson, S. (1992). A consumer values orientation for materialism and its measurement: Scale development and validation. *Journal of Consumer Research*, 19(3), 303.

Rook, K. S. (1984). Promoting social bonding: Strategies for helping the lonely and socially isolated. *American Psychologist*, 39(12), 1398–1407.

2　Knowing there is a trap at hand

2.1 How do we know there is a trap?

The purpose of this book is to establish the theory of the MLH trap and ways to untangle it. This requires systematically exploring and elaborating the relevant constructs for understanding the MLH trap and discovering other potentially significant constructs that may contribute to constituting a theory, a research agenda and guidelines for consumers to cushion themselves against the trap. Since the main purpose is theory-building and advancement, identifying the path to craft the theory becomes the foremost task. Therefore, a comprehensive literature search process is followed to identify, integrate and propose the theory of the trap. The resultant theoretical framework attempts to establish relationships among the constructs, which are further stated in formal propositions. The constructs are related to consumer values and choices and the surrounding environment. Therefore, the *level of analysis* is the individual consumer. The study is an analysis of the academic literature employing *systematic review* for the purpose of identifying gaps in the literature and areas that need to be worked on.

Any marketer knows there is an issue that arises when the consumer starts feeling the effects of materialism and exhibiting it verbally or through their consumption practices. Consumer satisfaction reportedly plummets when they are unable to gain the satisfaction and happiness promised in marketing communications. This inability causes frustration which can either be translated into more consumption to fill the gap or outright rejection of the product. Enhanced consumption may be temporarily beneficial to the marketer but triggers more problems for consumers; as it is the onset of the MLH trap. Eventually a reaction of dislike of the marketed product will emerge, reducing both the level of consumption and, more importantly, consumer happiness.

2.2 Systematic literature review

The objective of theory development is progress in academic understanding that is comprehensive, systematic and largely based on scientific search of the literature. *Content analysis* is the systematic qualitative approach to obtaining the content of communication in the form of proposition through various media (Krishnaswamy et al., 2013). Multiple methods can be used for content analysis in establishing a comprehensive review of the constructs. A *systematic literature* review is a form of content analysis using one category of media, that is, academic literature. This book follows the technique of the five-step systematic review advocated by Kidder et al. (1981). The five steps and the process are now discussed.

2.2.1 Choosing the phenomenon

The main phenomenon explored in this book is materialism, whereas the three main constructs of interest are materialism, loneliness and happiness. All other contingent factors revolve around materialism and its relationship to other constructs.

2.2.2 Media selection for systematic literature search

The media selected for the systematic review is academic journals (articles only) and related books. Initial screening is based on the complete range of existing literature on materialism. However, the analysis is focused

Table 2.1 Selected top-tier journals with greater content on materialism constructs

Full name of journal	Code
1 *American Psychologist*	AP
2 *Journal of Applied Social Psychology*	JASP
3 *Journal of Consumer Policy*	JCP
4 *Journal of Consumer Psychology*	JCPsy
5 *Journal of Consumer Research*	JCR
6 *Journal of Happiness Studies*	JHS
7 *Journal of Marketing Research*	JMR
8 *Journal of Personality and Social Psychology*	JPSP
9 *Journal of the Academy of Marketing Science*	JAMS
10 *Personality and Individual Differences*	PID
11 *Psychological Inquiry*	PI
12 *Psychology & Marketing*	P&M
13 *Social Indicators Research*	SIR
14 *Journal of Social Psychology*	JSP

only on academic articles from journals specific to consumer behaviour and consumer policy. The 14 journals selected for analysis are identified primarily on the basis of impact factor and secondly on high relevance to the constructs of interest in the search process. These journals represent tier-1 journals, ensuring high-quality content selection. The EBSCOhost and PsycINFO databases and the journals' websites were used to access the targeted journals and the relevant articles. The focus is on articles only, and book reviews, discussions, mails and introductions to special issues are excluded. The list of journals is presented in Table 2.1, along with the abbreviations selected for analysis; the journals have high impact factors and a high percentage of content pertaining to the constructs of interest.

Given the multidisciplinary variation in materialism research, some additional journals were included in the search process, such as *Psychological Science, Emotion, Human Relations, European Journal of Consumer Psychology* and *North American Journal of Psychology*. Besides the journal articles, prominent books on *consumer behaviour*, materialism, loneliness and happiness were also included in the search process. A detailed list of articles selected from different journals is given in the Appendix.

2.2.3 Coding categorization

The sample obtained is coded according to the categorization of the journals and the constructs of interest. The selected journals are coded using numbered integers 1–14 and given abbreviations; the next most relevant journals are numbered 15–19, and all other journals containing only a few articles on the constructs of interest are numbered 20. The constructs are then coded using their acronyms. The coding categorization of the constructs and selected journals is given in Appendix 7.1A.

2.2.4 Sampling strategy

In order to obtain a sample the population is estimated through a key word search of the scholarly articles. One search engine (Google Scholar) and two databases (EBSCOhost and PsycINFO) were used for the purposes of estimating the population, that is, available academic literature on materialism and related constructs. The following eight key words were used for the literature search across all three sources: 'materialism', 'materialism and happiness', 'materialism and loneliness', 'materialism and social support', 'materialism and green consumption', 'materialism and well-being', 'loneliness and happiness', 'materialism, loneliness and happiness'. Table 2.2 shows the details for each key word search for the databases. It shows a total

Table 2.2 Key word search results from main search engines*

Key words	Google Scholar		EBSCOhost		PsycInfo
	General	SV	General	SV	SV
Materialism	327,000	–	39,831	–	2,001
Materialism and well-being	27,300	36	28,781	63	145
Materialism and happiness	80,200	150	5,210	26	81
Materialism and loneliness	21,300	40	1,245	5	–
Materialism and green consumption	43,900	14	4,097	5	3
Materialism and social support	163,000	1	18,148	1	95
Loneliness and happiness	96,200	122	7,365	27	165
Materialism-loneliness-happiness	23,000	–	462	–	–
Total	**781,900**	**363**	**105,139**	**127**	**2,490**

SV = Specific to Variables

*Retrieved December 2015

of 781,900 articles on materialism. The databases confirm the availability of articles that were searched through Google Scholar.

The sample for analysis from this huge number of articles is obtained by following a systematic procedure which employs four steps. These include key word search, author search, search of future citations of related papers, references to the most-cited papers and searching/reviewing of related books. There are two primary focus points in conducting the sampling process. One is the sources and predictors of materialism as a consumer value. The other is the outcomes of materialism and their impact on the happiness and well-being of the consumer. There is an effort to identify the moderators/mediators of the materialism-loneliness trap and the eventual contributors to sustained happiness.

Rather than making the review an all-inclusive endeavour and an exhaustive summary of materialism literature, the multidimensional extant materialism literature is synthesized and integrated according to the following four techniques, such that it is covered in a systematic way and the possibility of inclusion of more constructs in the theoretical framework is enhanced for future research. The sequential steps led to the uncovering of further relevant sources. In total, the final sample includes 1170 journal articles from the selected journals, 363 articles from other sources and search engines and 18 books with relevant chapters. The structure of the review is modelled on other reviews in the field of marketing and consumer behaviour. The following four steps elaborate the search process and subsequent sampling.

2.2.4.1 Key word search

A key word search is carried out for the top journals of consumer behaviour on the basis of their high impact factor and relevance to the constructs of interest. It includes both marketing and non-marketing journals. The details are encapsulated in Table 2.3.

The purpose of the key word search is to summarize the breadth of the materialism literature in selected journals. The analysis, however, is focused upon variables that moderate/mediate materialism's relationship with loneliness and happiness and is narrowed down from the materialism literature. The sampling process is carried out in two phases whereby in the first phase 363 articles identified from the search engine are browsed

Table 2.3 Frequency and percentage of materialism-related literature in selected journals*

Journal	M	The other variables with M						LH
		WB	H	L	GC	SS	LH	
American Psychologist	13	4	3	1	0	5	0	3
Journal of Applied Social Psychology	16	4	5	1	5	1	0	2
Journal of Consumer Policy	19	0	16	1	0	2	0	2
Journal of Consumer Psychology	61	4	11	1	16	29	0	2
Journal of Consumer Research	65	14	10	2	5	34	0	10
Journal of Happiness Studies	106	20	32	4	4	43	3	85
Journal of Marketing Research	115	13	30	2	7	62	1	13
Journal of Personality and Social Psychology	21	1	3	1	11	5	0	6
Journal of the Academy of Marketing Science	95	38	15	0	8	34	0	1
Personality and Individual Differences	147	61	21	9	3	53	0	0
Psychological Inquiry	98	35	22	4	5	30	2	27
Psychology & Marketing	31	15	7	4	5	0	0	2
Social Indicators Research	313	107	78	11	19	94	4	94
Journal of Social Psychology	70	1	8	1	3	57	0	49
Total	**1170**	**317**	**261**	**42**	**91**	**449**	**10**	**296**
Percentage presence of constructs		**27.1**	**22.3**	**3.6**	**7.8**	**38.4**	**0.9**	

M = Materialism, WB = Well-being, H = Happiness, L = Loneliness, GC = Green Consumption, SS = Social Support

*Retrieved December 2015

to enhance understanding of materialism as a construct and in the second phase *1170 selected journal articles* are browsed to enhance understanding of the impacts of materialism and to identify contingency factors.

There is a very low percentage presence of literature on the materialism-loneliness relationship, about 3.6%, and almost negligible literature on the relationship between materialism, loneliness and happiness (about 0.9%). This suggests further probing and research is required. A detailed description of the presence of each construct in selected journals is given in Appendix 7.1B.

Abstracts of the identified articles from the selected journals are browsed to check relevance to understanding and unfolding the materialism-loneliness-happiness trap. The details of the procedure are shown in Table 2.4. The total number of articles from marketing journals is 386 while 784 articles are from non-marketing journals. Only 27%, i.e., 313 articles from the total of 1170, pertain to the MLH trap.

Table 2.4 Frequency of articles relevant to the MLH trap in selected journals*

Full title of journal	Marketing		Total	Relevant to MLH trap	
	Yes	No		Frequency	%
American Psychologist		√	13	4	31
Journal of Applied Social Psychology		√	16	6	38
Journal of Consumer Policy	√		19	17	89
Journal of Consumer Psychology	√		61	12	20
Journal of Consumer Research	√		65	12	18
Journal of Happiness Studies		√	106	39	37
Journal of Marketing Research	√		115	33	29
Journal of Personality and Social Psychology		√	21	4	19
Journal of the Academy of Marketing Science	√		95	15	16
Personality and Individual Differences		√	147	30	20
Psychological Inquiry		√	98	28	29
Psychology & Marketing	√		31	11	35
Social Indicators Research		√	313	93	30
Journal of Social Psychology		√	70	9	13
Total	**386**	**784**	**1170**	**313**	**27**

MLH = Materialism-Loneliness-Happiness

Relevant to the MLH trap = MWB+MH+ML+MLH

*Retrieved December 2015

2.2.4.2 Author search

On the basis of the search already carried out, the most notable authors in the field of materialism were identified. These are authors who have published numerous works in the field of materialism and other consumer-related values and impacts over the years. The process helped obtain a sample based on a frequency count of citations and number of published articles, providing an integrated list of 37 authors who have contributed significantly to materialism theory, as shown in Appendix 7.1C. In the search process only those authors whose articles were cited by more than 100 published articles and which are most relevant to materialism and other constructs of interest were included. The details of the author search process are shown in Appendix 7.1D.

2.2.4.3 Most frequently cited articles covering materialism

The journal articles sampled in 'key word' and 'author' search helped in accumulating journal articles having the highest number of citations. The high number of citations provides an indicator of quality, relevance and popularity. The resultant sample includes journal articles that are frequently cited, also shown in Appendix 7.1D.

2.2.4.4 Recent citations of related papers

The identification of notable authors provides only a snapshot of the important contributions to already established theory. However, a higher number of citations is sometimes due to the number of years that have passed since publication (the older the article the higher the chances of its being cited). This may provide the theoretical basis for emerging models, but not for new insights into materialism theory. Therefore it is important to look into future citations of notable articles, investigating related variables, such that different theoretical possibilities can be sought.

Accounting for the possibility of major or related contributions with a lesser number of citations (less than 100) is covered by looking at future citations of the most frequently cited articles. Then, given the multidisciplinary variation in materialism research, some articles from journals other than the selected journals are also included in the sample. The details of these are shown in Appendix 7.1E.

2.2.4.5 Review of related books

Prominent books on consumer behaviour, materialism, loneliness and happiness are also included in the sample. The purpose is to review the established and base literature regarding the variables and their theoretical underpinnings. The details of the sample of books are given in Appendix 7.1F.

In summary, the sampling process was carried out in a two-phase sequential process, which helped in finding further relevant academic material. In total, 1170 journal articles were sampled from the selected journals, 363 articles were selected from other sources and search engines and 18 books were identified for the final sample. From the total articles 386 were from marketing journals while 784 articles were from non-marketing journals. The abstracts of the articles were browsed in general to understand materialism as a construct and the related MLH trap along with the contingency factors of the trap. Only 313 articles from the total pertain to the trap. Then the most notable authors in the field of materialism were identified on the basis of recurrence and articles with more than 100 citations. The process helped obtain a sample of 36 authors contributing significantly to the materialism theory based on a frequency count of citations and number of published articles. The high number of citations provides an indicator of quality, relevance and popularity and may provide the theoretical basis for emerging models. However new insights into the materialism theory may not be attained with this approach. Therefore it is important to look at future citations of notable articles as well. So, in order to accommodate the possibility, major or related contributions with a lesser number of citations (less than 100) were also included in the final sample.

2.3 Theory-building process

The theory-developing process is carried out in the following steps as established by Bacharach (1989), Suddaby (2010) and Sutton and Staw (1995).

2.3.1 Conceptual definitions of the constructs

The development process of any theory begins with clear conceptual definitions of the constructs such that each construct crystallizes with a unique conceptual identity manifesting its own features and dimensions. The three main constructs of the study, i.e., materialism, loneliness and happiness, have been well established, defined and operationalized in earlier academic endeavours and have been used in the same way. Social support, religiosity and nostalgia have also been well operationalized. However, environmentalism, social giving and dimensions of the purchase mechanism have been well defined but not operationalized as a variable for any materialism-related analytical study. The current research utilizes the established definition of these constructs, though for some of the constructs operationalization needs further advancement in future research.

2.3.1.1 Materialism

The definition of materialism given by Richins and Dawson (1992) is followed by the current research; it is described as a craving for worldly possessions as a steering value of life. It has been operationalized with three aspects of materialism, namely, *centrality*, *happiness* and *success*. Complete definitions of the constructs are given in Table 2.4.

2.3.1.2 Loneliness

The definition of loneliness is given by Rook (1984) and Gordon (1976) and is followed by the current research; it is described as a relatively persistent experience of emotional suffering. It has been operationalized under three categories, namely isolation, relational connectedness and communicational connectedness.

2.3.1.3 Happiness

The definition of happiness is given by Fave et al. (2011) and is followed by the current research; it describes happiness as a measure of psychological and subjective well-being and a satisfied state of mind. It has been operationalized into three different related mechanisms, which are positive affect, the absence of negative affect and satisfaction with life as a whole (Lu, 1999).

The other three constructs of social support, nostalgia and religiosity have been defined and operationalized in various academic researches. However, social giving, environmentalism and purchase mechanisms have been used in research but not operationalized fully for research on materialism and consumer behaviour.

2.3.2 Boundary assumptions and identification of the scope

Overall materialism theory is multidimensional and multidisciplinary. The existing research focuses only on the trap of materialism and loneliness and the consequential loss of happiness, establishing its scope. It does not address exhaustively the impacts of materialism on the consumer.

The trap revolves around consumers who have made themselves lonely due to an over-emphasis on material gratification in an attempt to make themselves happy, but who end up lonely, unhappy and dissatisfied. The solution provided by the theory of the MLH trap concentrates on interventions into the social (social support, religiosity and social giving) and psychological (environmentalism, nostalgia and consumption patterns) factors of the consumer. It does not focus on the economic and demographic

Table 2.5 Conceptual definitions of the constructs

Construct	Definition	Ref.
Materialism	A craving for worldly possessions as a steering value of life that ensures happiness and success in a materialist's belief. It has three aspects namely, *centrality* (major goal in life is acquiring worldly possession), *happiness* (quest for material goods is the primary source of satisfaction), and *success* (worldly possessions act as indicator of success to others).	Richins & Dawson, 1992
Loneliness	A relatively persistent experience of emotional suffering caused by rejection or exclusion by others from a social group, being misunderstood and alienated, lacking suitable and desirable social partners for various activities, specifically events that furnish prospects for intimacy and a sense of communal integration.	Rook, 1984
	A perception that the quantity, significance and the quality of social relationships do not meet the social needs of an individual.	Gordon, 1976
Happiness	A state of mind that results from being eudemonically and hedonically satisfied. It is composed of positive affect, absence of negative affect and satisfaction with life as a whole.	Fave et al., 2011
Social support	An amalgam of factors that create the perception that one is cared for, will receive help and assistance from others and is a participant in a supportive social network. It has four properties namely, content (meanings given to the relationships), directedness (relationships and their reciprocity), intensity (level of binding and obligation) and frequency (level of interactions).	Kaplan et al., 1977
Environmentalism	The practice of consuming less or recycled products, compromising on price, convenience, brand and performance to highlight environmental sustainability concerns and principles.	Pepper et al., 2009
Religiosity	The level of influence of religion on the philosophy and principles of life, daily activities, praying, religious services and routine.	Wilkes et al., 1986
Social giving	The practice of being benevolent, giving and sharing with others. It is a form positive social behaviour.	Bartal, 1976
Nostalgia	A sentimental longing for the past and memories accompanied by pleasure and sadness. It is a prevalent experience, and draws on uniquely human cognitive abilities.	Wildschut et al., 2010

factors of the consumer or account for consumer motives, thus setting the boundaries for the research.

Moreover the research focuses on conscious efforts of the consumer to curb materialism. It does not deal with changes in materialism due to the passage of time, economic systems and other cultural factors. The theory is established and discussed in section 6.2, with elaboration of the scope and boundary assumptions.

2.3.3 Identifying, defining and establishing the contingency factors

Various factors are identified as contingency factors that can moderate or mediate the given relationship between the primary variables of materialism-loneliness-happiness. Social support is identified as moderating both relationships, that is, it weakens the materialism-loneliness trap and strengthens the negative relationship between loneliness and happiness.

Pro-environmental or green consumption, socio-centric and experiential purchases and religious orientation moderate the relationship between materialism and loneliness. Then, factors such as social giving are identified to impact between loneliness and happiness. Religiosity and environmentalism are also seen to have an impact upon predispositions to materialism and the development of materialistic orientations.

Definitions are given above in Table 2.5, whereas the direction of relationships is given in the sections on theory advancement and the research agenda, sections 6.3, 6.4, 6.5 and 6.6.

2.3.4 Theoretical framework and future directions

The last and the most important step in the theory-building process is the development of the theoretical framework based upon the identified constructs and the contingency factors, set within the constraints of the boundary assumptions and established scope. The theory of sustained happiness for loneliness-stricken materialists, i.e. the Socio-Psychological Theory of the Materialism Trap, is at this point established, with its contingencies for untangling the trap, within the given boundary assumptions, and is discussed in detail in Chapter 6. Future research directions and agenda are discussed in Chapter 7.

References

Bacharach, S. B. (1989). Organizational theories: Some criteria for evaluation. *Academy of Management Review*, 14(4), 496–515.

Bartal, D. (1976). *Prosocial behavior: Theory and research*. Washington, DC: Hemisphere Publishing Corporation.

Fave, D. A., Brdar, I., Freire, T., Vella, B. D., and Wissing, M. P. (2011). The eudaimonic and hedonic components of happiness: Qualitative and quantitative findings. *Social Indicators Research*, 100 (2), 185–207.

Gordon, S. (1976). *Lonely in America*. New York, NY: Simon and Schuster.

Kaplan, B. H., Cassel, J. C., and Gore, S. (1977). Social support and health. *Medical Care*, 15(5), 47–58.

Kidder, L. H., Wrightman, S., and Cook, T. D. (1981). *Research Methods in Social Relations*. 4th edition. London, UK: Holt, Rinehart and Winston.

Krishnaswamy, K. N., Sivakumar, A. I., and Mathirajan, M. (2013). *Management Research Methodology: Integration of Principles, Methods and Techniques*. 9th edition. New Delhi, India: Pearson Education, South Asia; Dorling Kindersley.

Lu, L. (1999). Personal or environmental causes of happiness: A longitudinal analysis. *Journal of Social Psychology*, 139(1), 79–90.

Pepper, M., Jackson, T., and Uzzell, D. (2009). An examination of the values that motivate socially conscious and frugal consumer behaviors. *International Journal of Consumer Studies*, 33, 126–136.

Richins, M. L., and Dawson, S. (1992). A consumer values orientation for materialism and its measurement: Scale development and validation. *Journal of Consumer Research*, 19(3), 303.

Rook, K. S. (1984). Promoting social bonding: Strategies for helping the lonely and socially isolated. *American Psychologist*, 39(12), 1398–1407.

Suddaby, R. (2010). Editor's comments: Construct clarity in theories of management and organization. *Academy of Management Review*, 35(3), 346–357.

Sutton, R. I., and Staw, B. M. (1995). What theory is not. *Administrative Science Quarterly*, 40(3), 371–384.

Wildschut, T., Sedikides, C., Routledge, C., Arndt, J. and Cordaro, F. (2010). Nostalgia as a repository of social connectedness: The role of attachment-related avoidance. *Journal of Personality and Social Psychology*, 98(4), 573–578.

Wilkes, R. E., Burnett, J. J., and Howell, R. D. (1986). On the meaning and measurement of religiosity in consumer research. *Journal of the Academy of Marketing Science*, 14(1), 47–56.

3 You may not know but you are already trapped!

3.1 Materialism – an intensifying consumer value

Materialism is a strong guiding sentiment or value that broadly reflects the importance an individual assigns to possessions, belongings and wealth (Belk, 1984). There are different views on materialism in consumer research, mainly funnelling into two broad categories of materialism either as a personality trait or a consumer value. Materialism, if taken as a trait, is an accumulation of certain personality traits that differentiates a materialist from a non-materialist, such as greed, resentment, self-centredness and lack of generosity, as defined by Belk (1984). However, Richins and Dawson (1992) consider materialism as a steering value of life that ensures happiness and success in a materialist's belief. Three aspects of materialism were identified by Richins and Dawson (1992) namely, *centrality* (major goal in life is acquiring worldly possessions), *happiness* (quest for material goods is the primary source of satisfaction), and *success* (worldly possessions act as an indicator of success to others). Therefore, materialists may neglect important social needs by making happiness and satisfaction conditional upon attainment of material goods, thereby promoting dissatisfaction.

Materialism is a universal, powerful phenomenon that can be witnessed across different cultures, irrespective of national prosperity levels (Ger and Belk, 1996). In the modern economy, characterized by high levels of consumerism and competition, materialism and its outgrowths have become central concerns in a consumer's life (Pieters, 2013). Moreover, Belk (1995) stated materialism to be a macro-level consumer behaviour issue that needs further study.

Kasser (2002) identified that materialists have a greater focus on extrinsic needs and motivation, such as possessions and success, but a weak emphasis on intrinsic needs and motivation, such as associations and connectivity with other people. As a result, materialists are less happy, less psychologically healthy and at a lower level of well-being. Materialists are inclined towards theming their lives around acquisition of money, possessions and belongings. For them happiness comes in this way, and is necessary to be successful in life (Richins and Dawson, 1992; Tybout and Artz, 1994; Yoon and Vargas, 2006). Such consumers view financial success as a significant life achievement compared to self-acceptance, affiliation or community fame (Kasser and Ryan, 2001). Materialism is associated with a weak image of 'self' that is externally regulated (Zhou and Gao, 2008). As the consumer exhibits a lower level of self-concept clarity and self-efficacy, with an external locus of control, they tend to show higher levels of materialism as a means of gaining control and self-enhancement (Watson, 2014). This is because the value of materialism opposes the values of conservatism, egalitarianism and harmony (Schwartz, 1999). Moreover, contrary to popular belief, materialism is not related to affluence or western values, rather is universal and found across consumer categories (Ger and Belk, 1996).

Burroughs et al. (2013) addressed the motivational perspectives of materialism, identifying that materialism is an outgrowth of a combination of unmet higher-order psychological needs, incomplete and dubious development of self-concept, and inability to form loving and close social relationships. As elucidated by motivational theory, consumers often try to conciliate unfulfilled core needs with material and prized possessions but such products are often meaningless substitutes, and are poorer motivations towards well-being (Deci and Ryan, 2000). There are four types of insecurities that lead to materialism, if elaborated from motivational theory perspective (Burroughs et al., 2013). These are: developmental insecurity (stems from childhood experiences and results in a shabby self-concept, usually explored under attachment theory), personal insecurity (likeliness to employ material goods as a means to assert control, fuel vanity and fill in gaps of self-assertion), social insecurity (uneasiness and distress with social relations and dealings leading to social anxiety) and existential insecurity (construction of intricate defence mechanisms to anticipate the existential aspects of life, one of which is materialism). These insecurities lead to higher levels of materialism. Moreover, family structure and socio-economic status also impacts the materialism levels of young family members. Adults reared in disruptive families are more materialistic and exhibit high levels of compulsive consumption, stress and general insecurities (Rindfleisch, Burroughs, and Denton, 1997).

In a nutshell, the existing literature supports materialism as a consistently intensifying consumer value in the global culture of consumerism that requires both theoretical and practitioner elaboration (Belk, 1995; Burroughs et al., 2013; Hurst et al., 2013; Watson, 2015).

3.1.1 Materialism as a negative consumer value

In order to evaluate whether materialism is socially irresponsible and a negative consumer value, there is a need to understand the overarching impact of materialism on consumers' lives, such that the claim can be legitimized (Muncy and Eastman, 1998). Interestingly, material possessions and their pursuit are a natural and healthy part of a consumer's routine. It is only when the pursuit of material possessions extends beyond the healthy point and interferes with other important aspects of consumer's life, such as reducing the importance of social relationships, that it is likely to become detrimental to the consumer as an individual and disintegrative for the society (Muncy and Eastman, 1998).

Materialism's negative effects spread to the consumer's workplace as well, as materialistic values tend to be associated with lower work ethics, lower work-related well-being (Deckop, Jurkiewicz, and Giacalone, 2010) and enhanced work–family conflict (Promislo et al., 2010). Work–family conflict often leads to stress in the personal life of the consumer (Promislo et al., 2010), acting as a void, which the consumer wishes to fill with materialism (Bauer et al., 2012).

Materialistic consumption does not make the consumer happier or more satisfied, implying that current consumerism is particularly ineffective in bringing happiness to the consumer (Caldas, 2010). When hedonism is practised without a sense of belonging and mastery, the balance is disturbed resulting in reduced perception of happiness (Caldas, 2010). Moreover, materialism is found to be positively related to peer influence and negatively related to the level of religiosity, economic socialization and impact of the mother's materialistic levels (Flouri, 1999).

Materialistic values disturb the social connectivity of the consumer (Bauer et al., 2012; Pieters, 2013; Kasser 2002) and motivate them towards self-centred consumption patterns. Moreover, Ruvio et al. (2014) examined the degree to which materialism worsens feelings of stress and anxiety in times of trouble for materialistic consumers. Generally, such consumers show higher levels of stress and engage in extensive impulsive purchasing and conspicuous consumption when faced with difficult or threatening situations, as suggested by terror management theory. Thus, materialistic consumers experience bad times to a greater extent than do less materialistic consumers (Ruvio et al., 2014).

The consumer's possessions reflect the materialistic values behind them as a highly materialistic consumer tends to prefer possessions that are high in prestige and status, are publicly consumed, are expensive, and are associated with important others (Richins, 1994). Moreover, these materialistic values do not occur in any consumer by chance but rather are developed and enhanced by the social influence of family and peers who promote a materialistic lifestyle along with personal values (Ahuvia and Wong, 2002).

Another negative consequence of endorsement of materialistic values is uncontrolled compulsive buying, which is a disruptive consumption behaviour and is regarded as a psychiatric disorder. Materialism and its endorsement in young adults are found to be the strongest predictors of impulsive buying (Dittmar, 2005), conspicuous consumption and brand loyalty (Podoshen and Andrzejewski, 2012).

Interestingly, at the same time, materialism also has a beneficial side for the consumer. If material possessions are used for the sheer joy of utilizing them, they can actually augment social connectivity (Pieters, 2013). Materialistic purchasing, especially hedonic or luxury consumption, reflects resourcefulness and can improve mood (Deci and Ryan 2000), decrease negativity and increase satisfaction with life through the spillover effect (Hudders and Pandelaere, 2012). However, the effect is not long lasting (Pieters, 2013) and is therefore outweighed by the negative impacts. This indicates that materialistic values are not to be shunned as altogether negative, but that they need to be channelized. There is a need to identify how the consumers can be trained to use them to their benefit and remain happy with their consumption.

Materialism may be regarded as both good and bad depending upon the way consumers evaluate their standard of living (Sirgy et al., 2013). When consumers use fantasy-based expectations (ideal standards) to compare and evaluate their standard of living, this leads to negative evaluation of the standard of living, leading to dissatisfaction with life (Sirgy et al., 2013). The dissatisfaction fuels the drive to gain more and more in life (Hsee et al., 2009). However, when consumers use reality-based expectations (standards based on ability) to evaluate their standard of living, they are likely to feel satisfied and do not feel the rush to continually acquire more in life (Sirgy et al., 2013). Moreover, self-esteem discrepancy increases materialism (Park and Deborah, 2011). There is a heightened desire in the consumer to self-enhance thorough other means if there is high explicit but low implicit self-esteem. Such consumers are outwardly confident but have a low level of self-worth and tend to follow eminent others or purchase illustrious products and indulge in materialistic consumption to cover this up (Park and Deborah, 2011).

Therefore, materialism as a value is comprised of several antecedents that are social, psychological and cultural in nature, and the extent to which the consumer is materialistic and their evaluation of materialism makes it a negative or positive tendency. The following figure shows the several antecedents of materialism that have been identified by various authors and compiled here for the purpose of theoretical advancement.

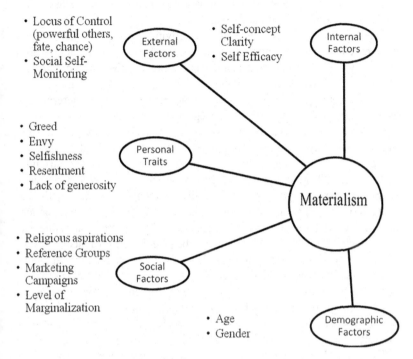

- Locus of Control (powerful others, fate, chance)
- Social Self-Monitoring

- Self-concept Clarity
- Self Efficacy

- Greed
- Envy
- Selfishness
- Resentment
- Lack of generosity

- Religious aspirations
- Reference Groups
- Marketing Campaigns
- Level of Marginalization

- Age
- Gender

Figure 3.1 Antecedents of materialism

3.1.2 Materialism and associated consumption patterns

A consumer's buying behaviour is a process based on six stages right from the recognition of need to post-purchase evaluation of the consumption made (Solomon et al., 2013). The actual purchase is just one part of the process. There are three factors relating to the consumer that impact the whole consumer-buying behaviour. These are personal, psychological and social factors. The personal factors are unique to the consumer such as age, gender, sex, race and family role. The psychological factors include motives, perception, ability and knowledge, personality, lifestyles and attitudes. The social factors are factors in the consumer's environment that influence the buying behaviour, including opinion leaders, family, reference groups, social class and culture (Kardes, Cronley and Cline, 2010; Solomon et al., 2013).

Prior research on materialism has focused only on the psychological factors of the consumer, specifically motives, personality and lifestyles, in determining the buying behaviour and its impacts. However, as the buying behaviour is an amalgam of all three factor types, there is a need to look beyond the psychological factors and include social factors to better evaluate the role and impact of materialism.

There are three types of discretionary activities that a consumer exhibits in the purchase process, namely material purchase, experiential purchase and creative activities to gain satisfaction and happiness (Millar and Thomas, 2009). These discretionary activities in the purchase process follow two types of consumption pattern, that is, egocentric purchase patterns and socio-centric purchase patterns. The egocentric purchase patterns signify conspicuous buying, creative activities and material purchases for self-gratification. They serve the ego-defensive function, making the consumer feel secure, esteemed and good about themselves (Kardes, Cronley and Cline, 2010). On the other hand, socio-centric purchase patterns signify inconspicuous buying, experiential purchases and community activities. Such activities strengthen social relationships, enhance social bonding, provide more opportunities to cherish relationships and improve social skills that can refine and soothe social affiliations. These remain to be postulated into a theory.

Egocentric and material purchases have a negative impact on happiness as consumers buy joyless material goods that provide comfort but fail to provide pleasure (Easterlin, 2007; Frank, 2004). Therefore, previous research suggested that the way to improve social relationships and well-being is to engage in dematerialization of lifestyle and to adopt a socio-centric consumption pattern. However, there is no empirical evidence to support the claim.

The purchase mechanism can thus be categorized into three parts. The first part is the factors that shape the purchase intention, reflecting the personal, psychological and social factors surrounding the consumer. The second is the purchase process, made up of six stages, and the third part is the discretionary activities (behavioural part) of the consumer, which can be patterned either ego-centrically or socio-centrically. These parts have been separately highlighted by different authors and have been consolidated in this study for the purpose of further elaboration.

According to Hudders and Pandelaere (2012), materialism can play an important part in constructing, maintaining, restoring and transforming social support networks. Social comparison theory suggests that as consumers compare and contrast their social and material standing with others on a continuous basis, luxury consumption based on social activities may bring happiness. Consumers can utilize such activities to enhance their appeal, make them more 'wanted' and fit in better with others (Belk, 2010). Furthermore, Tsang et al. (2014) identified that luxury consumption not only fortifies materialistic lifestyle, it also leads to positive mood enhancement (Deci and Ryan, 2000) and increase in life satisfaction, leading to happiness.

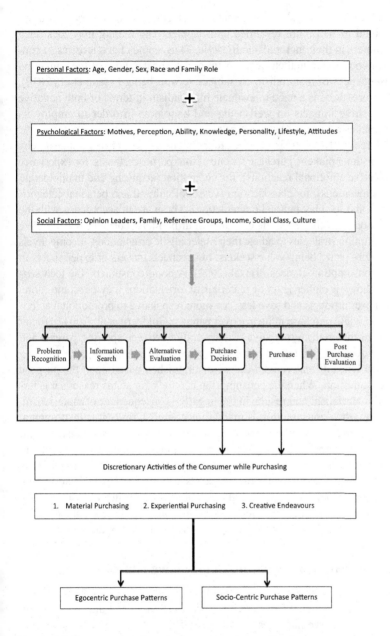

Figure 3.2 Consumer purchase precursors, process and patterns

Specifically, in the short run, materialists engaged in luxury consumption tend to feel more rewarded and happier. The feeling may lock such consumers in their materialistic lifestyle. Thus, some characteristics of consumption may strengthen materialism and alleviate some of the damaging consequences of materialism on subjective well-being (Tsang et al., 2014). Therefore, there is a need to evaluate materialism in terms of both negative and positive impacts on well-being and happiness in order to employ its potential as a sustainable source of happiness.

Moreover, Holt (1995) identified four dimensions of consumption, whereby the consumer makes a purchase for one of four purposes, that is: for experience (subjective emotional reactions), for integration (acquiring and manipulating object meanings), for classification (vessel of cultural and personal categorization) and for play (autotelic interaction). These are in accordance with the discretionary activities of the consumer. Furthermore, consumers also utilize consumption strategies to adjust their materialistic orientations, income levels and future plans, being value seekers, big spenders, savers or experiencers in their consumption choices (Tatzel, 2003). Among consumers, the teen segment shows a higher level of materialistic orientation; they consume more, buy newer products and save less, are more responsive to promotional activities and wield purchase influence over parents (Goldberg et al., 2003). Higher levels of materialism may give rise to conflict between spouses, parents and family over consumption decisions (Larsen, Sirgy, and Wright, 1999).

Two types of materialism can be distinguished based upon the purpose of consumption. When the consumption is purely for status reasons it is terminal materialism and results in the negative consequences of materialism, whereas when consumption is made to accomplish tasks it is instrumental materialism and results in the beneficial consequences of materialism (Scott, 2009). Nevertheless, only the consumption process is positively related to subjective well-being and happiness as it displays increased possibilities for satisfying various consumption needs when provided with additional giving opportunities. However, the relationship may not remain positive when other aspects of consumer motives are considered such as the relative, symbolic and hedonic dimensions of consumption (Royo, 2008).

3.2 Materialism as an approach to gaining happiness

Materialism is a consumer value that has its roots in consumption motives and is used as a signal for status and success (Solomon et al., 2013). Many consumers believe happiness to be dependent upon material goods (Hsee et al., 2009; Caldas, 2010). Therefore, such consumers arrange their lives around the attainment and possession of material goods and prized valuables and thereby exhibit high levels of materialism (Pieters, 2013). Conversely, materialism seldom contributes to happiness over a sustained period of time. A number of studies have identified that materialism is inversely related to psychological well-being. It has been found to have a negative relationship with self-actualization (Kasser and Ahuvia, 2002), and with life satisfaction and self-esteem (Richins and Dawson, 1992), and a positive relationship with anxiety and the proportion of time spent unhappy and depressed (Kasser and Ahuvia, 2002). Furthermore, if consumers highly emphasize materialistic pursuits, they tend to be less happy with their personal lives and act in ways that are socially and ecologically damaging (Kasser, 2006).

3.2.1 Happiness and subjective well-being

Happiness is a measure of psychological and subjective well-being. It is a state of mind that results from eudemonic and hedonic satisfaction (Fave et al., 2011). It is an amalgam of factors including personality traits such as self-esteem, extraversion, optimism and self-control, the time frame in which happiness is being measured, and the life role being played at any point of time. It is sensitive to fortune and adversity. Most researchers agree that happiness is likely to be composed of three related mechanisms: positive affect, the absence of negative affect and satisfaction with life as a whole (Lu, 1999). On the other hand subjective well-being in itself is a construct related to optimum experiencing and functioning of the individual. Again the hedonic aspect focuses on pleasure attainment and pain avoidance while the eudemonic approach focuses on higher-degree realization of the self and exploration of potentials (Ryan and Deci, 2001). Happiness as a trait is reflected and predicted through feeling good about the self, excitement, pride, sociability and activeness, as well as being in the conditions for gaining experiences (Csikszentmihalyi and Hunter, 2003). Happiness and satisfaction with life should both be understood as outcomes of the interactive process between the personal characteristics of the consumer and the socio-economic factors that surround them (Haller and Hadler, 2006).

Therefore, happiness is a deeper-level emotional feeling and is relative to the overall subjective well-being of a consumer. It is important to evaluate it at a finer level to assess the current and sustained level of a consumer's happiness (Hsee et al., 2009). Subjective well-being has not been found to be directly proportional to a high level of income, money or materialistic pursuits (Diener and Biswas-Diener, 2002). In relation to materialism, three kinds of hedonic experiences are particularly important in relation to bringing happiness to the consumer. These are monetary experience (consumer's feeling about a specific sum of money), acquisition experience (feelings of a consumer when buying) and consumption experience (feelings of a consumer while consuming and utilizing the bought product). Monetary experiences are relative and the consumer compares them with external reference points and products. The happiness depends upon the relative monetary value for the consumer. Acquisition experiences are based on cognitive face information and are also relative. The happiness depends upon the relative desirability of the product. Consumption experiences are, however, personal and absolute. Therefore, the happiness depends upon personal desire as well as the consumption and actual use of the product (Hsee et al., 2009).

It is assumed in general that happiness depends upon absolute levels of wealth and acquisition. However, happiness and well-being can never be truly indicated by economic measures alone, especially at an upper level of societal development (Diener and Seligman, 2004). Moreover, behavioural theorists argue that if the consumer shifts attention towards the consumption experience rather than money and acquisition itself, this will improve the satisfaction level with the consumption, making consumer happier (Diener and Biswas-Diener, 2002; Hsee et al., 2009). Accordingly, enduring happiness can be reached through hedonic adaptation, that is, affective sensitization after experiencing something for some time (Diener, Lucas, and Scollon, 2006). Consumers should focus upon variable events and experiences (adaptation resistant) rather than fixed events and experiences (adaptation prone) to ensure enduring happiness (Hsee et al., 2009; Kurtz, Wilson, and Gilbert, 2007). There is also a growing debate regarding the way in which materialism is adopted in a consumer's daily routine. If adopted appropriately, materialism may not disrupt consumption activities, making the consumer unhappy and dissatisfied (Simms and Potts, 2012). The consumer will not become a victim of lack of happiness or dissatisfaction if they learn to develop longer and lasting relationships with the material possessions, i.e. focusing on recycling, re-growing, re-employing and even re-imagining the ways in which material goods can be used and shared. Secondly, becoming more active in life and developing useful skills can help the consumer being happier. Lastly, sharing the things a consumer owns can bring happiness (Simms and Potts, 2012).

Demographic factors account for only small variations in the level of happiness of a consumer compared to environmental factors, social skills, leisure activities and religiosity (Argyle, 2003). Therefore, studies on consumer happiness should also reflect on other causes and correlates.

3.2.2 Materialism and happiness

A consumer indulges in materialistic purchase to achieve a higher level of self-esteem and to delight themselves with the happiness of consumption (Bauer et al., 2012; Richins and Dawson, 1992). However, the feeling is usually temporary. When the consumer eventually realizes materialistic goal incongruity it leads to sadness and despair, as the ideal state of happiness is never reached, due to its relative comparison (Soscia, 2007). Moreover, Tatzel (2003) also identified that acquiring material goods only to enhance social standing decreases well-being and happiness.

High levels of materialism usually reflect a negative relationship with life satisfaction, well-being and happiness (Ahuvia and Wong, 1995; Belk, 1985; Diener and Oishi, 2000; La Barbera and Gürhan, 1997; Richins and Dawson, 1992). It is, however, just one part of the consumer's larger value system. Burroughs and Rindfleisch (2002) identified that even as a small part of the value system materialism has a great impact on the well-being and happiness of the consumer because of its opposition to collectivistic values such as family and religion. The resultant tension caused by this opposition decreases well-being and satisfaction, which ultimately leads to lower levels of happiness. The effect is especially pronounced for consumers with high collectivistic values but who look for power and achievement at the same time (Burroughs and Rindfleisch, 2002).

Eaton and Eswaran (2009) divided material products into Veblen goods (leisure or luxury products), standard private goods and standard public goods. In affluent societies it is perceived that with greater income the consumer can easily concentrate upon Veblen goods and achieve a higher level of happiness. In reality, as overall productivity increases, the consumption level of luxury goods rises, crowding out non-Veblen goods (private and public) and regressing the general well-being of the consumer and society (Eaton and Eswaran, 2009). So, with greater concentration on materialistic purchase and consumption, well-being and happiness are negatively affected.

Standard of living has a greater impact on a consumer's happiness when the consumer exhibits a higher level of materialism (Huang and Rust, 2011). This is because maintenance of a higher standard of living is instrumental in gaining happiness for materialistic consumers (Sirgy, 1998). In the event of not being able to maintain a high living standard, the desired level of happiness is not achieved.

Materialistic consumption does not automatically ensure happiness (Caldas, 2010; Hsee et al., 2009). It is merely a perception of a consumer with high materialistic values that greater consumption and material possessions ensure success, status and esteem relative to others (Kasser and Ryan, 2001; Richins and Dawson, 1992; Tybout and Artz, 1994). The unfulfilled motive generally leads to stress, marginality and a feeling of incompleteness (Bauer et al., 2012; Kasser, 2002; Pieters, 2013).

3.2.3 Facets of materialism and happiness

A materialistic consumer indulges in consumption in ongoing pursuit of a perceived level of happiness. The consumer desires to be happy through material possessions rather than through relationships or accomplishments in life (Richins and Dawson, 1992). They anticipate that happiness comes with more material possessions, which are often exhibited to incite envy or show plenty. Instead the possessions depict a void (Bauer et al., 2012). As the ideal state is never accomplished, the pursuit of happiness and the exhibition of possession-defined success leads to a feeling of despair.

In further studies by Pieters (2013), based on the three facets of materialism discussed by Zhou and Gao (2008), the author identified that materialism could be divided into three distinct subtypes. The first is *possession-defined success*, which is about social comparison. It signifies success as an instrument to impress others and is often used as a status signal. The second is *acquisition as pursuit of happiness*, which reflects the deficiency in the ideal state of the consumer. There is a temporal comparison between a present sub-optimal state and a better state of ownership in the future. The third is *acquisition centrality*, which is about enjoying luxury consumption and the pure delight of buying and having material possessions. It represents material 'mirth' or hedonistic values.

Whenever consumers utilize material goods as a status signal or as a proxy measure of happiness, expectation is not fulfilled. Instead, the level of unhappiness and despair increases, as it arises out of extrinsic goal motivation (Kasser, 2002). This happens because of the crowding-out effect initiated by over-emphasis on material possessions and a substitution effect that occurs between relationships (group values and goals) and material goods (individual values and goals). The material goods crowd out the rational spaces for relationships and push them away, emphasizing the 'self' for the consumer. Therefore, materialism shows a strong positive relationship with impulse buying, conspicuous consumption and brand loyalty (Podoshen and Andrzejewski, 2012). Eventually despair and hostility fill the void created by this substitution (Pieters, 2013; Watson, 2015).

Materialism is found to be negatively related to happiness and the eight domains of life satisfaction, and all three facets are also found to be negatively related to domains of quality of life satisfaction (Ahuvia and Wong, 1995; Roberts and Clement, 2007; Ryan and Dziurawiec, 2001). Both 'possession-defined success' and 'acquisition as the pursuit of happiness' are found to be strongly negative while 'acquisition centrality' is slightly negative (Roberts and Clement, 2007). Similarly, Watson (2015), in a facet-level analysis of materialism and the five-factor model of personality. It identified that materialism correlates strongly with neuroticism and low agreeableness in general. In particular, possession-defined success was predicted by low modesty and self-consciousness. Acquisition as the pursuit of happiness was predicted by low straightforwardness and vulnerability and acquisition centrality was predicted by anxiety and low modesty. All identified factors give rise to lower levels of satisfaction with life and resultantly lower levels of happiness.

The third facet of materialism, representing material mirth, that is, acquisition centrality or hedonic consumption, displays a different relationship with well-being and level of loneliness. It increases connectivity and happiness (Pieters, 2013). This happens because it arises out of intrinsic motivation providing consumers with control and autonomy as they indulge in hedonic or luxury consumption. When the consumer indulges in luxury consumption without extrinsic or ulterior motives, this provides happiness for the consumer. The discovery provides a silver lining in relation to the appraisal of materialism as merely a negative consumer value (Tsang et al., 2014). The effects, however, are relatively temporary (Soscia, 2007). Moreover, unrestrained materialism may lead to reduced happiness; nonetheless, it can also play the role of rebalancing the equation by strengthening the support networks of the consumer (Hudders and Pandelaere, 2012). This reflects the requisites for understanding how and in what ways materialism could be modified to achieve a higher level of happiness.

3.3 Materialism as forerunner of loneliness

3.3.1 Materialism and loneliness

Loneliness can be best defined as a relatively persistent experience of emotional suffering caused by rejection or exclusion by others from a social group, being misunderstood and alienated, or lacking suitable and desirable social partners for various activities, specifically the events that furnish prospects for intimacy and a sense of communal integration (Rook, 1984).

Loneliness occurs when there is a perception that the quantity, significance and quality of social relationships do not meet the social needs of an individual (Gordon, 1976). It is often accompanied by a stressful feeling. The characteristics of loneliness include the experiencing of distress and feelings of marginality, anxiety and aversion accompanied by sadness (Rubinstein, Shaver, and Peplau, 1979). Loneliness can be thought of as the social equivalent of physical pain, thirst or hunger, whereby the mere perception of social isolation or exclusion motivates the individual towards the formation and continuous maintenance of social relationships (Hawkley and Cacioppo, 2010).

A wide body of research has enumerated the physical and health problems associated with loneliness, such as heart problems, Alzheimer's disease and sleep deprivation, and problematic health issues related to stress and depression, such as high blood pressure and premature death (Hawkley et al., 2010; Seeman, 2000). Such health issues can result in decreased ability to self-regulate, which can hamper the normal social functioning of an individual (Hawkley and Cacioppo, 2010). Loneliness has a temporal characteristic, whereby some individuals may feel it only for a brief period while others may experience tenacious loneliness that may disrupt life (Young, 1982).

McWhirter (1990) analyzed the previous research on dimensions of loneliness and identified that most authors follow the dimensions acknowledged by Young (1982). These are: chronic (persistent isolation due to personal deficiencies), situational (disruption in relationship pattern) and transient (occasional feeling of loneliness) loneliness. In simpler form Weiss (1987), identified two types of loneliness: emotional loneliness (lack of attachment relationship) and social loneliness (deficient social network).

Materialistic values of self-enhancement such as hedonism, power and achievement can damage the quality of connectedness, as they are opposed to both the self-transcendence values such as benevolence and social values such as family and community orientation (Kilbourne, Grünhagen, and Foley, 2005; Schwartz, 1992). Materialism decreases the ability to fulfil the social needs of connectivity and intimacy (Kasser, 2002). The significance that materialists assign to acquiring material goods has a detrimental effect on their social relationships (Lane, 2000). According to Pieters (2013), materialism contributes to loneliness and vice versa but to varying degrees, forming a self-perpetuating cycle. Materialism crowds out the social relationships of an individual, making them indulge in such consumption patterns that social and intimate relationships are left behind (Bauer et al., 2012; Kasser, 2002; Larsen, Sirgy, and Wright, 1999; Pieters, 2013).

There can be different social, psychological, economic and environmental determinants of loneliness. By far the biggest contribution to the acceleration of loneliness is made by the pursuit of materialistic goals (Kasser, 2002). According to attachment theory whenever basic needs of intimacy and connectivity (primary attachment) are not fulfilled, there is a natural tendency to resort to compensations or substitutes based upon material possessions (secondary attachments) (Deci and Ryan, 2000; Mikulincer and Shaver, 2008). The values and goals that individuals pursue have a significant impact on their well-being (Deci and Ryan, 2000). As materialism is one of the outgrowths of extrinsic goal motivation, involving the unrestrained attainment of material goods (Kasser 2002), it eventually accelerates loneliness.

The research literature identifies four types of loneliness intervention: (1) Enhancement of social skills, (2) Provision of social support, (3) Incrementation of social interaction opportunities and (4) Curing of maladaptive social cognition (Hawkley and Cacioppo, 2010). Enhancement of social skills can play a major role in the reduction of loneliness. Likewise, materialism could be motivated towards satisfying the need for relatedness. The problem with achieving a re-socialized self is that most consumers who are already lonely fail to reconnect to others due to 'anxious coping' arising from fear of rejection (Mikulincer and Shaver, 2008). According to the self-determination theory, such consumers do not develop a materialistic lifestyle for reasons of self-esteem or self-portrayal, or for their own sake. Rather they attach themselves to material possessions, either to reflect success or in pursuit of happiness, actually trying to avoid the pain of social isolation (Pieters, 2013). So, the social connections such consumers desire to establish remain suspended and preferences are never expressed due to fear of rejection. Moreover, females exhibit acquisition centrality more than males, suggesting they are more fearful of an event of social isolation (Ryan, Kalil, and Leininger, 2009). This suggests that following the onset of the materialism-loneliness cycle, it is more difficult to break free for men.

Materialism resides in psychological aspects of the consumer relating to motives, values and lifestyle. Loneliness resides in social aspects of the consumer relating to family, group influences, social class and culture. Any attempt to break free of the cycle entails intervention into both the psychological and social aspects of the consumer, requiring a theoretical construction of both domains.

3.3.2 Relationship of materialism and loneliness to happiness

A consumer indulges in different sorts of consumption behaviours in pursuit of happiness. These consumption behaviours encompass material purchase, experiential purchase and creative endeavours (Howell and Hill, 2009; Millar and Thomas, 2009). However, the effort to gain happiness is seldom satisfied, because in an attempt to buy happiness through material purchases, the consumer socially isolates themselves and has no one to share the joy of purchase with. Thus the pursuit of happiness remains a pursuit, even though the consumer has spent a lot to gain that happiness. Having no answer and not being able to attain what is wished for, despair and discontent start to fill the void created by happiness goal incongruity.

The constant pursuit of happiness of a materialistic consumer renders them lonely and isolated as they cherish and value personal comfort and happiness more than the sharing of comfort and happiness with others (Mauss et al., 2012). In other words, they want to be happy but not to share this happiness with others. The major reason behind this, as defined by the *attitude function theory*, is the focus on materialistic purchases, which play an ego-defensive function for the consumer, making them feel safe, secure and esteemed (Kardes, Cronley, and Cline, 2010). The consumer feels that it is the materialistic purchases which will make them esteemed and craved for. Others will look up to them and will be around them to venerate them. In reality, however, materialism disturbs the connectivity of the consumer with others. The message is not translated well to others. As consumers feel lonely, negative affect is enhanced and positive affect is decreased, resulting in unhappiness. The major cause of this is the consumer's inability to affirm their capability of developing happy, fulfilling relationships (Dyer, 2010). Such consumers feel that it is materialistic valuables that will build up relationships for them. On the contrary it is the consumer themselves who must affirm the ability to build happy, long-lasting relationships (Dyer, 2010).

Therefore, there is a need to determine consumption patterns that allow the consumer opportunities to share the joy and utility of purchases with others and also to cherish the purchase personally. It is important to subdue the relationship between material goods and social connectivity. Connectivity should be based on a consumer's social behaviour and not on their material reserves. Otherwise, materialism enhances loneliness and decreases life satisfaction, which results in a continued feeling of despair and unhappiness (Ang et al., 2014), thus keeping the spiral running.

References

Ahuvia, A. C., and Wong, N. Y. (2002). Personality and values based materialism: Their relationship and origins. *Journal of Consumer Psychology*, 12(4), 389–402.

Ahuvia, A., and Wong, N. (1995). Materialism: Origins and implications for personal well-being. *European Advances in Consumer Research*, 2, 172–178.

Ang, C. S., Mansor, A. T., and Tan, K. A. (2014). Pangs of loneliness breed material lifestyle but don't power up life satisfaction of young people: The moderating effect of gender. *Social Indicators Research*, 117(2), 353–365.

Argyle, M. (2003). 18 Causes and Correlates of Happiness. *Well-being: The Foundations of Hedonic Psychology*, 353.

Bauer, M. A., Wilkie, J. E., Kim, J. K., and Bodenhausen, G. V. (2012). Cuing consumerism: Situational materialism undermines personal and social well-being. *Psychological Science*, 23(5), 517–523.

Belk, R. W. (2010). Sharing. *Journal of Consumer Research*, 36(5), 715–734.

Belk, R. W. (1995). Collecting as luxury consumption: Effects on individuals and households. Journal of Economic Psychology, 16(3), 477–490.

Belk, R. W. (1985). Materialism: Trait aspects of living in the material world. Journal of Consumer Research, 265–280.

Belk, R. W. (1984). Three scales to measure constructs related to materialism: Reliability, validity and relationships to measures of happiness. Advances in Consumer Research, 11(1), 291–297.

Burroughs, J. E., and Rindfleisch, A. (2002). Materialism and well-being: A conflicting values perspective. Journal of Consumer Research, 29(3), 348–370.

Burroughs, J. E., Chaplin, L. N., Pandelaere, M., Norton, M. I., Ordabayeva, N., Gunz, A., and Dinauer, L. (2013). Using motivation theory to develop a transformative consumer research agenda for reducing materialism in society. *Journal of Public Policy and Marketing*, 32(1), 18–31.

Caldas, S. B. (2010). The happiness-to-consumption ratio: An alternative approach in the quest for happiness. *Estudios Gerenciales*, 26(116), 15–35.

Csikszentmihalyi, M., and Hunter, J. (2003). Happiness in everyday life: The uses of experience sampling. *Journal of Happiness Studies*, 4(2), 185–199.

Deci, E. L., and Ryan, R. M. (2000). The 'what' and 'why' of goal pursuits: Human needs and the self-determination of behavior. *Psychological Inquiry*, 11(4), 227–268.

Deckop, J. R., Jurkiewicz, C. L., and Giacalone, R. A. (2010). Effects of materialism on work-related personal well-being. *Human Relations*, 63(7), 1007–1030.

Diener, E., and Biswas-Diener, R. (2002). Will money increase subjective well-being? *Social Indicators Research*, 57(2), 119–169.

Diener, E., and Oishi, S. (2000). Money and happiness: Income and subjective well-being across nations. *Culture and Subjective Well-Being*, 185–218.

Diener, E., and Seligman, M. E. (2004). Beyond money: Toward an economy of well-being. *Psychological Science in the Public Interest*, 5(1), 1–31.

Diener, E., Lucas R. E., and Scollon, C. N. (2006), Beyond the hedonic treadmill: Revising the adaptation theory of well-being. *American Psychologist*, 61(4), 305–314.

Dittmar, H. (2005). Compulsive buying–a growing concern? An examination of gender, age, and endorsement of materialistic values as predictors. *British Journal of Psychology*, 96(4), 467–491.

Dyer, W. W. (2010). Real Magic: Creating Miracles in Everyday Life. UK: Harper Collins.

Easterlin, R. A. (2007). The escalation of material goals: Fingering the wrong culprit. *Psychological Inquiry*, 18(1), 31–33.

Eaton, B. C., and Eswaran, M. (2009). Well-being and affluence in the presence of a veblen good*. *Economic Journal*, 119(539), 1088–1104.

Fave, D. A., Brdar, I., Freire, T., Vella, B. D., and Wissing, M. P. (2011). The eudaimonic and hedonic components of happiness: Qualitative and quantitative findings. *Social Indicators Research*, 100(2), 185–207.

Flouri, E. (1999). An integrated model of consumer materialism: Can economic socialization and maternal values predict materialistic attitudes in adolescents? *Journal of Socio-Economics*, 28(6), 707–724.

Frank, R. H. (2004). How not to buy happiness. *Daedalus*, 133(2), 69–79.

Ger, G., and Belk, R. W. (1996). Cross-cultural differences in materialism. *Journal of Economic Psychology*, 17(1), 55–77.

Goldberg, M. E., Gorn, G. J., Peracchio, L. A., and Bamossy, G. (2003). Understanding materialism among youth. *Journal of Consumer Psychology*, 13(3), 278–288.

Gordon, S. (1976). *Lonely in America*. New York, NY: Simon and Schuster.

Haller, M., and Hadler, M. (2006). How social relations and structures can produce happiness and unhappiness: An international comparative analysis. *Social Indicators Research*, 75(2), 169–216.

Hawkley, L. C., and Cacioppo, J. T. (2010). Loneliness Matters: A theoretical and empirical review of consequences and mechanisms. *Annals of Behavioral Medicine*, 40(2), 218–227.

Hawkley L. C., Thisted R. A., Masi C. M., and Cacioppo J. T. (2010). Loneliness predicts increased blood pressure: Five-year cross-lagged analyses in middle-aged and older adults. *Psychology and Aging*, 25(3), 132–141.

Holt, D. B. (1995). How consumers consume: A typology of consumption practices. *Journal of Consumer Research*, 1–16.

Howell, R. T., and Hill, G. (2009). The mediators of experiential purchases: Determining the impact of psychological needs satisfaction and social comparison. *Journal of Positive Psychology*, 4(6), 511–522.

Hsee, C. K., Yang, Y., Li, N., and Shen, L. (2009). Wealth, warmth, and well-being: Whether happiness is relative or absolute depends on whether it is about money, acquisition, or consumption. *Journal of Marketing Research*, 46(3), 396–409.

Huang, M. H. and Rust, R. T. (2011). Sustainability and consumption. *Journal of the Academy of Marketing Science*, 39(1), 40–54.

Hudders, L., and Pandelaere, M. (2012). The silver lining of materialism: The impact of luxury consumption on subjective well-being. *Journal of Happiness Studies*, 13(3), 411–437.

Hurst, M., Dittmar, H., Bond, R., and Kasser, T. (2013). The relationship between materialistic values and environmental attitudes and behaviors: A meta-analysis. *Journal of Environmental Psychology*, 36, 257–269.

Kardes, F. R., Cronley, M. L., and Cline, T. W. (2010). *Consumer Behavior: Science and Practice*. South-Western Cengage Learning.

Kasser, T. (2006). Materialism and its alternatives. *Contributions to Positive Psychology*, 200.

Kasser, T. (2002). The Value of Materialism: A Psychological Inquiry. Cambridge, MA: MIT Press.

Kasser, T., and Ahuvia, A. (2002). Materialistic values and well-being in business students. *European Journal of Social Psychology*, 32(1), 137–146.

Kasser, T., and Ryan, R. M. (2001). Be careful what you wish for: Optimal functioning and the relative attainment of intrinsic and extrinsic goals. *Life Goals and Well-being: Towards a Positive Psychology of Human Striving*, 116–131.

Kilbourne, W., Grünhagen, M., and Foley, J. (2005). A cross-cultural examination of the relationship between materialism and individual values. *Journal of Economic Psychology*, 26(5), 624–641.

Kurtz, J. L., Wilson, T. D. and Gilbert, D. T. (2007). Quantity versus uncertainty: When winning one prize is better than winning two. *Journal of Experimental Social Psychology*, 43(6), 979–985.

La Barbera, P. A., and Gürhan, Z. (1997). The role of materialism, religiosity, and demographics in subjective well-being. *Psychology and Marketing*, 14(1), 71–97.

Lane, R. E. (2000). *The Loss of Happiness in Market Democracies*, New Haven, CT: Yale University Press.

Larsen, V., Sirgy, M. J., and Wright, N. D. (1999). Materialism: The construct, measures, antecedents, and consequences. *Academy of Marketing Studies Journal*, 3(2), 78–110.

Lu, L. (1999). Personal or environmental causes of happiness: A longitudinal analysis. *Journal of Social Psychology*, 139(1), 79–90.

Mauss, I. B., Savino, N. S., Anderson, C. L., Weisbuch, M., Tamir, M., and Laudenslager, M. L. (2012). The pursuit of happiness can be lonely. *Emotion*, 12(5), 908.

McWhirter, B. T. (1990). Loneliness: A review of current literature, with implications for counseling and research. *Journal of Counseling and Development*, 68(4), 417–422.

Mikulincer, M., and Shaver, P. R. (2008). 'Can't buy me love': An attachment perspective on social support and money as psychological buffers. *Psychological Inquiry*, 19(3–4), 167–173.

Millar, M., and Thomas, R. (2009). Discretionary activity and happiness: The role of materialism. *Journal of Research in Personality*, 43(4), 699–702.

Muncy, J. A., and Eastman, J. K. (1998). Materialism and consumer ethics: An exploratory study. *Journal of Business Ethics*, 17(2), 137–145.

Park, J. K., and Deborah, R. J. (2011). More than meets the eye: The influence of implicit and explicit self-esteem on materialism. *Journal of Consumer Psychology*, 21(1), 73–87.

Pieters, R. (2013). Bidirectional dynamics of materialism and loneliness: Not just a vicious cycle. *Journal of Consumer Research*, 40(4), 615–631.

Podoshen, J. S., and Andrzejewski, S. A. (2012). An examination of the relationships between materialism, conspicuous consumption, impulse buying, and brand loyalty. *Journal of Marketing Theory and Practice*, 20(3), 319–334.

Promislo, M. D., Deckop, J. R., Giacalone, R. A., and Jurkiewicz, C. L. (2010). Valuing money more than people: The effects of materialism on work–family conflict. *Journal of Occupational and Organizational Psychology*, 83(4), 935–953.

Richins, M. L. (1994). Special possessions and the expression of material values. *Journal of Consumer Research*, 522–533.

Richins, M. L. (1994). Valuing things: The public and private meanings of possessions. *Journal of Consumer Research*, 21(4), 504–521.

Richins, M. L., and Dawson, S. (1992). A consumer values orientation for materialism and its measurement: Scale development and validation. *Journal of Consumer Research*, 19(3), 303.

Rindfleisch, A., Burroughs, J. E., and Denton, F. (1997). Family structure, materialism, and compulsive consumption. *Journal of Consumer Research*, 312–325.

Roberts, J. A., and Clement, A. (2007). Materialism and satisfaction with over-all quality of life and eight life domains. *Social Indicators Research*, 82(1), 79–92.

Rook, K. S. (1984). Promoting social bonding: Strategies for helping the lonely and socially isolated. *American Psychologist*, 39(12), 1398–1407.

Royo, M. (2008). Consumption and subjective wellbeing: Exploring basic needs, social comparison, social integration and hedonism in Peru. *Social Indicators Research*, 89(3), 535–555.

Rubinstein, C. N., Shaver, P., and Peplau, L. A. (1979). Loneliness. *Human Nature*, 2(2), 58–65.

Ruvio, A., Somer, E., and Rindfleisch, A. (2014). When bad gets worse: The amplifying effect of materialism on traumatic stress and maladaptive consumption. *Journal of the Academy of Marketing Science*, 42(1), 90–101.

Ryan, L. and Dziurawiec, S. (2001). Materialism and its relationship to life satisfaction. *Social Indicators Research*, 55(2), 185–197.

Ryan, R. M. and Deci, E. L. (2001). On happiness and human potentials: A review of research on hedonic and eudaimonic well-being. *Annual Review of Psychology*, 52(1), 141–166.

Ryan, R. M., Kalil, A., and Leininger, L. (2009). Low-income mothers' private safety nets and children's socioemotional well-being. *Journal of Marriage and Family*, 71(2), 278–297.

Schwartz, S. H. (1999). A theory of cultural values and some implications for work. *Applied Psychology*, 48(1), 23–47.

Schwartz, S. H. (1992). Universals in the content and structure of values: Theoretical advances and empirical tests in 20 countries. *Advances in Experimental Social Psychology*, 25(1), 1–65.

Scott, K. (2009). Terminal materialism vs. instrumental materialism: Can materialism be beneficial? Doctoral dissertation, Oklahoma State University.

Seeman, T. (2000). Health promoting effects of friends and family on health outcomes in older adults. *American Journal of Health Promotion*, 14(6), 362–370.

Simms, A., and Potts, R. (2012). *The New Materialism*. London, UK: bread, print & roses.

Sirgy, M. J. (1998). Materialism and quality of life. *Social Indicators Research*, 43(3), 227–260.

Sirgy, M. J., Gurel-Atay, E., Webb, D., Cicic, M., Husic-Mehmedovic, M., Ekici, A, and Johar, J. S. (2013). Is materialism all that bad? Effects on satisfaction with material life, life satisfaction, and economic motivation. *Social Indicators Research*, 110(1), 349–366.

Solomon, M. R., Baboosy, G. J., Askegaard S. T., and Hogg, M. K. (2013). *Consumer Behaviour: A European Perspective*. 5th edition. Harlow, UK: Pearson.

Soscia, I. (2007). Gratitude, delight, or guilt: The role of consumers' emotions in predicting post-consumption behaviors. *Psychology and Marketing*, 24(10), 871–894.

Tatzel, M. (2003). The art of buying: Coming to terms with money and materialism. *Journal of Happiness Studies*, 4(4), 405–435.

Tsang, J. A., Carpenter, T. P., Roberts, J. A., Frisch, M. B., and Carlisle, R. D. (2014). Why are materialists less happy? The role of gratitude and need satisfaction in the relationship between materialism and life satisfaction. *Personality and Individual Differences*, 64, 62–66.

Tybout, A. M., and Artz, N. (1994). Consumer psychology. *Annual Review of Psychology*, 45 (1), 131–169.

Watson, D. C. (2015). Materialism and the five-factor model of personality: A facet-level analysis. *North American Journal of Psychology*, 17(1), 133.

Watson, D. C. (2014). A model of the materialistic self. *North American Journal of Psychology*, 16(1), 137.

Weiss, R. S. (1987). Reflections on the present state of loneliness research. *Journal of Social Behavior and Personality*, 2(2), 1.

Yoon, S., and Vargas, P. T. (2006). On the psychology of materialism: Wanting things, having things, and being happy. *Advertising and Society Review*, 7(1).

Young, J. E. (1982). *Loneliness, Depression and Cognitive Therapy: Theory and Application*. New York, NY: Wiley.

Zhou, X., and Gao, D. G. (2008). Social support and money as pain management mechanisms. *Psychological Inquiry*, 19(3–4), 127–144.

4 The beginning of the materialism-loneliness-happiness (MLH) trap

4.1 Understanding the MLH trap

The materialism-loneliness trap crystallizes out of the consumer's motivations towards materialism and consumption. It is initiated by the crowding-out effect of materialism, whereby the consumer indulges in such consumption patterns that social and intimate relationships are left behind (Bauer et al., 2012; Kasser 2002; Pieters, 2013). Material goods gain more importance than social relationships and become the major external motivation in life. This means the consumer surrounds themselves with material goods, leaving no space for social affiliations and relationships. When the consumer eventually perceives loneliness, they indulge in more consumption, trying to create a feel-good factor, using material goods as a substitution feature (Pieters, 2013). The consumer is thus trapped in a cycle where the lonelier they feel, the more they indulge in materialism as a coping strategy, and the lonelier they become due to the crowding-out effect of materialism. As a result, even after indulging in materialistic consumption the consumer remains unhappy and dissatisfied with the goods purchased. This is because of the lack of sharing prospects for the lonely consumer.

Materialism and loneliness both contribute to perpetuating the other, but to varying degrees, forming a vicious cycle (Pieters, 2013). Although a lonely consumer may or may not employ materialism as a coping strategy to lessen the despair attached to loneliness, nonetheless a materialistic consumer will eventually fall prey to loneliness due to its crowding-out effect. Therefore, materialism causes loneliness to a greater degree than loneliness causes materialism (Pieters, 2013). Once trapped in the cycle it becomes increasingly difficult for the consumer to break free of it. This is because the remedy they utilize, that is, increased consumption and self-gratification, in itself entails materialism and loneliness (Mikulincer and Shaver, 2008; Pieters, 2013; Ryan, Kalil, and Leininger, 2009). A loneliness-stricken materialist consumer disturbs his social connectivity and

Figure 4.1 The materialism-loneliness-(un)happiness trap

sharing prospects. Soon they realize internally there is no one to share the happiness of the consumption with. The dissatisfaction from this realization makes them discontented with the purchases and they frequently switch, sell, resell and exchange products and brands in an attempt to get satisfaction. In effect, satisfaction from purchase and happiness from consumption is rarely achieved because the consumer's value system and motivations have already been disturbed.

4.2 Breaking away from the trap

When the consumer finally starts to feel the effect of running after material possessions and sacrificing social ties and happiness in the process, there is a realization that something is wrong. However, usually the consumer is unable to understand what went wrong and where, and struggles to find a way out.

4.2.1 Social support as an important factor in loosening the MLH trap

It seems that once materialism sets its roots in the daily lives of consumers, loneliness and unhappiness will eventually shadow in. However, there are other factors that may dispel the negative spiral. One of these is the social support network of a consumer. Social support is the amalgam of factors that create the perception that one is cared for, will receive help and assistance from others, and is a participant in a supportive social network. Social support has four interactional properties namely: *content* (meanings given to the relationships including rituals, values, beliefs, self-esteem, expressions and the like), *directedness* (relationships and their reciprocity), *intensity* (level of binding and obligation) and *frequency* (level of interactions) (Kaplan, Cassel, and Gore, 1977).

There are two forms of social support, real and perceived, which are present at different levels of society and provide different functions. At the general and external level, the community develops and initiates social identity and a sense of belonging. At the next level, social networks are formed through social relationships such as in the family, workplace and neighbourhood. Finally, at the most specific and internal level, is relational intimacy, the development of a feeling of commitment, responsibility and well-being (Lin et al., 2013). So, the community, social network and intimate friends provide three types of social supports, that is, instrumental, emotional and informational support, leading to psychological well-being (Lin et al., 2013; Ryan et al., 2009; Tardy, 1985; Zimet et al., 1988). Thus, lack of support from community and friends, family and intimate partner increases social loneliness, family loneliness and romantic loneliness respectively. If the three types of social support are analyzed, it is seen that loneliness (social, family and romantic) is more effectively reduced by emotional support, compared to the other types. Moreover, emotional support was found to increase well-being (Mendieta, Martín, and Jacinto, 2013). Loneliness has been associated with lower reported well-being (Mellor et al., 2008). Intimate relationships and social networks have a stronger association with well-being than does community support.

Several studies report an inverse relationship between social support and loneliness (Ginter, Glauser, and Richmond, 1994; Weiss, 1987; Young, 1982). Perception of loneliness can result in decreased subjective well-being (Mendieta, Martín, and Jacinto, 2013). It was observed that the level and form of social support determine the type and level of loneliness and that they have an inverse relationship. However, at the same time social support mediates the relationship between loneliness and subjective well-being, with subjective well-being reduced when loneliness prevails (Mendieta, Martín, and Jacinto, 2013).

There can be different social, psychological, economic and environmental determinants of loneliness. A major role in the acceleration of loneliness and endorsement of materialism is played by people's motivations and values. The values and goals that individuals pursue have a significant impact on their well-being (Deci and Ryan, 2000). As materialism is one of the outgrowths of extrinsic goal motivation, involving the unrestrained acquirement of worldly possessions (Kasser, 2002), pursuing materialistic goals eventually accelerates loneliness.

Research also suggests that materialists have lower levels of social support, as they are less likely to value relationships. They also show lower satisfaction with their friends and their family lives (Richins and Dawson, 1992). A lack of social support may give rise to a feeling of general insecurity that may be a forerunner of materialistic values (Christopher et al., 2004). Similarly, it was identified by La Barbera and Gürhan (1997) that social support accounts for the negative relationship between materialism and subjective well-being. Materialism is often used as a coping mechanism, denying feelings of insecurity (Chang and Arkin, 2002) and as a mechanism for dealing with insecurity and anxiety (Christopher et al., 2004).

Zhou and Gao (2008) studied the mediating role of social support in greater depth. According to them both money and social support act as buffers against social pain (exclusion and loneliness). The moment an individual anticipates social exclusion, the desire for social support and materialism is heightened (Mikulincer and Shaver, 2008).When social support fails as a buffer, individuals often rely on materialistic pursuits, as a secondary buffer, to furnish the pain-reducing function. As a result, desire for social relationships is diminished, thereby reducing individual well-being (Zhou and Gao, 2008).

Materialism in its own way refurbishes and balances social support. Thus, materialism may lead to the restoration of social support by enhancing social acceptance (Ahuvia, 2008). Materialism may help to achieve societal goals while promoting significant social relationships (Zhou and Gao, 2008), although it may not be contributing to happiness (Ahuvia, 2008). Money can play an important part in constructing, maintaining, restoring and transforming social support networks (Ahuvia, 2008; Hudders and Pandelaere, 2012).

When it comes to loneliness, Hawkley and Cacioppo (2010) identified four types of loneliness that can be cured through improved social skills. Enhancement of social skills has shown the most remarkable results in clinical interventions for loneliness. Therefore, improved social skills can play a major role in the reduction of loneliness. Likewise, materialism could be motivated to satisfy the need for relatedness.

Thus the literature suggests that social support lessens the general insecurities of a materialistic consumer and reduces the anxiety and despair arising out of loneliness. However, as discussed, materialism resides in psychological aspects of the consumer relating to their motives, values and lifestyle, whereas loneliness resides in social aspects of the consumer relating to their family, group influences, social class and culture. Therefore social support can play an important role in mitigating loneliness as the consumer gains prospects for sharing the joy of material purchase and being happy. However, the happiness is usually temporary because there are other contingencies that impact materialism levels, pointing towards the deeper psychological aspects of the consumer. So, any attempt to break free of the cycle entails intervention into both the psychological and social factors of the consumer to allow the happiness gained to be sustainable.

4.2.2 Sustaining the level of happiness

In order to sustain the level of happiness the consumer needs to participate actively and be conscious of the purchase process (Burroughs et al., 2013; Carter and Gilovich, 2010; Goodman and Irmak, 2013; Huang and Rust, 2011;

Watson, 2014). Several longitudinal studies have revealed that conscious changes in psychological need satisfaction orientations and intervention into relative focus on life goals can effectively reduce emphasis on materialistic goals and values and increase well-being or happiness (Kasser et al., 2014). Research literature identifies social giving, experiential consumption, green consumption, active environmentalism, religiosity and planned-purchase decision-making as means of reducing materialistic motives and sustaining the level of happiness. Moreover, Chancellor and Lyubomirsky (2011) discussed the ways in which the consumer can shift away from materialistic orientations and still derive more hedonic pleasure from the consumption, stressing the importance of thrift. A consumer can achieve this by reducing debts, stretching positive experiences through appreciation and savouring, rekindling experiences through variation and nostalgic pondering, renting out products for use rather than buying, and resolutely pursuing intrinsic appreciation (Chancellor and Lyubomirsky, 2011).

Previous research suggested that the way to improve social relationships and well-being is to engage in dematerialization of lifestyle. However, in an era of intensifying consumerism, this demand seems absurd. The new approach emphasizes the 'resocialization' of lifestyle and consumption patterns. According to Belk (2006), money, as a representation of materialism, can play an important part in constructing, maintaining, restoring and transforming social support networks. There are many things that individuals can possess that can enhance their appeal and make them more 'wanted', and help them fit in with others (Belk, 2010). Furthermore, Tsang et al. (2014) identified that luxury consumption fortifies materialistic lifestyle. Luxury consumption leads to positive mood enhancement and increase in life satisfaction. The benefits of luxury consumption are enhanced and more rewarding for materialists, specifically in the short term. This elevated feeling may lock such consumers into their materialistic lifestyle. Thus, some characteristics of consumption may strengthen materialism and alleviate some of the damaging consequences of materialism on subjective well-being. Some activities that are related to consumption may be more rewarding to and available only to materialists (Tsang et al., 2014).

The problem with achieving a re-socialized self is that most individuals who are already lonely usually fail to reconnect with people due to 'anxious coping' out of fear of rejection (Mikulincer and Shaver, 2008). They do not develop a material lifestyle for self-esteem or self-portrayal, or for their own sake, but rather attach themselves to material possessions in an attempt to avoid the pain of social isolation (Pieters, 2013). So the social connections that such individuals are looking to establish in reality remain suspended. The preferences of such consumers are never expressed socially, due to fear of rejection. Moreover as materialism reduces consumer independence in the purchase process, the consumer is locked into consumption for the purpose of showing off to others and not for self-satisfaction, resulting in only temporary happiness (Goldsmith and Clark, 2012). However, the fears at the back of the consumer's mind keep them dissatisfied with the purchase process.

Howell and Hill (2009) found that among the two purchase types, experiential and material, experiential purchases exhibited increased connectivity and reduced signs of comparison. According to Pieters (2013), 'possessions can be important stores of social memories (souvenirs), tools of social protection (house), connection (phone), or production (family dinner table)'. Socio-centric motivations are enhanced by the relishing of particular social possessions, which can improve the effectiveness of social relationships (Richins, 1994). Experiential purchases are superior to material purchases as they tend to be more resilient to hedonic adaptation, that is, the loss of ability to deliver happiness (*positive affect*) as time passes. Moreover, experiential purchases make consumer happier as they are open to positive reinterpretations, are resilient to adverse comparisons and foster stronger social relationships (Van Boven, 2005). The experiences gained not only provide immediate delight, gratification and psychological nourishment but can be relived, relished and recreated.

Weinberger and Wallendorf (2008) differentiated between two types: material purchases that give rise to economic capital that can be shared or showed off to others, and experiential purchases that give rise to cultural capital that cannot be shared but can be relived and passed on. Consumers usually adapt slowly to experiential purchases as compared to material purchases, which can lead to both greater happiness and greater unhappiness with experiential purchases (Nicolao, Irwin, and Goodman, 2009). Material purchases, on the other hand quickly lose their pleasurable aspects due to the fast rate of adaptation, confining the materialistic consumer to a persistent search for more purchases to obtain that inner satisfaction (Burroughs et al., 2013; Dunn, Gilbert, and Wilson, 2011). Thus, the literature suggests that there is a need to move from ego-centric materialistic purchase to socio-centric purchase patterns based on experiences or socialization activities for a sustained level of happiness.

When consumption decisions are made, experiential purchases have a greater tendency to make consumers happy as compared to material purchases (Van Boven and Gilovich, 2003). This is because experiences are difficult to compare and evaluate and the happiness acquired is absolute, not relative (Hsee et al., 2009; Carter and Gilovich, 2010). On the other hand, material purchases are comparable and are usually evaluated on price, features, utilities and usage by reference group. Additionally the un-chosen option is considered long after the purchase has been made, leading to decreased satisfaction (Carter and Gilovich, 2010). Moreover consumers use maximizing strategy when purchasing material goods and use satis-ficing strategy when purchasing experiential goods (Carter and Gilovich, 2010; Shwartz, 2004).

Two factors have been identified that achieve consumption pattern changes in conscious consumers, namely environmental sacrifice and chari-table aid (Huang and Rust, 2011). Both factors contribute positive psychic benefits to consumers, creating a feel-good factor for them and contributing to happiness. Higher quality-of-life concerns and environmental awareness shift the focus of the consumer from material acquisitions to non-material aspects (Pepper et al., 2009), and the consumer becomes willing to consume less and compromise on price, brand, product features and performance. The value of materialism may be replaced with the value of conservation, ensuring that the consumption is in accordance with such principles, enhanc-ing the utility even with a lower level of absolute consumption. Moreover, Burroughs et al. (2013) identified pro-social giving and charitable aid as a means to reduce materialistic orientations.

Non-materialistic goods, including generic goods and green products, provide certain consumption benefits over materialistic goods, such as health, safety, symbolism and the internal concept of happiness (Ottman et al., 2006). As consumption decisions are translated from consumers' core needs and values, purchasing, recycling and reducing waste by means of green or pro-environment products and services leads to heightened self-esteem. It generates a feel-good factor for the consumer, in that they feel they are among those who care for the environment, a feeling that provides satisfaction (Flatters and Willmott, 2009; McDonald et al., 2009; Thogersen and Crompton, 2009). A higher willingness on the part of the consumer to undergo material sacrifice for the preservation of the environment through green or ethical consumption brings a sense of justice that loosens the grip of consumerism (Huang and Rust, 2011). Moreover, Kaplan (2000) advocates a higher state of altruism through the reasonable person model of motivation, which can facilitate the adoption of environmentally responsible consump-tion behaviour. It implies a movement from intrinsic motivation to extrinsic motivation that is socially responsible. It is important because materialistic beliefs decrease environmental concerns and impact environmental behav-iour negatively (Kilbourne and Pickett, 2008). Similarly, Sheth, Sethia and Srinivas (2011) proposed the concept of mindful consumption, which can act as a guiding principle for a consumer with a mindset of caring for self, the community and nature. Mindful consumption can translate into purchas-ing behaviours that counteract the excesses of materialistic consumption.

Materialistic consumers often focus on having or possessing new, expen-sive multi-feature products pertaining to prestige and status rather than using them (Goodman and Irmak, 2013). Such consumers fail to evaluate their actual feature usage rate before purchasing multi-feature expensive products, creating dissatisfaction with the purchase. If consumers evaluate their product usage rate and requirements before the purchase decision and focus on using rather than having products, it can positively enhance purchase satisfaction. This can lead to a lesser focus on acquisition and a greater focus on utility, bringing more value to purchase decisions (Goodman and Irmak, 2013). As a result the level of satisfaction and happiness achieved can be sustained over a longer period of time.

According to Dyer (2010), happiness does not lie within extravagant events, excessive consumption and extraordinary miracles that are out of a consumer's control. Rather happiness may come from small daily events handled in such a way that they become miracles. Wisdom lies in overcoming the materialistic urge and substituting it with careful consumption that is planned and calculated.

References

Ahuvia, A. C. (2008). If money doesn't make us happy, why do we act as if it does? *Journal of Economic Psychology*, 29(4), 491–507.

Bauer, M. A., Wilkie, J. E., Kim, J. K., and Bodenhausen, G. V. (2012). Cuing consumerism: Situational materialism undermines personal and social well-being. *Psychological Science*, 23(5), 517–523.

Belk, R. W. (2010). Sharing. *Journal of Consumer Research*, 36(5), 715–734.

Belk, R. (2006). Money as civilizing ritual. *Behavioral and Brain Sciences*, 29(2), 180.

Burroughs, J. E., Chaplin, L. N., Pandelaere, M., Norton, M. I., Ordabayeva, N., Gunz, A., and Dinauer, L. (2013). Using motivation theory to develop a transformative consumer research agenda for reducing materialism in society. *Journal of Public Policy and Marketing*, 32(1), 18–31.

Carter, T. J., and Gilovich, T. (2010). The relative relativity of material and experiential purchases. *Journal of Personality and Social Psychology*, 98(1), 146.

Chancellor, J., and Lyubomirsky, S. (2011). Happiness and thrift: When (spending) less is (hedonically) more. *Journal of Consumer Psychology*, 21(2), 131–138.

Chang, L., and Arkin, R. M. (2002). Materialism as an attempt to cope with uncertainty. *Psychology and Marketing*, 19(5), 389–406.

Christopher, A. N., Victoria Kuo, S., Abraham, K. M., Noel, L. W., and Linz, H. E. (2004). Materialism and affective well-being: The role of social support. *Personality and Individual Differences*, 37(3), 463–470.

Deci, E. L., and Ryan, R. M. (2000). The 'what' and 'why' of goal pursuits: Human needs and the self-determination of behavior. *Psychological Inquiry*, 11(4), 227–268.

Dunn, E. W., Gilbert, D. T., and Wilson T. D. (2011). If money doesn't make you happy, then you probably aren't spending it right. *Journal of Consumer Psychology*, 21(2), 115–125.

Dyer, W. W. (2010). *Real Magic: Creating Miracles in Everyday Life*. New York, NY: Harper Collins.

Flatters, P., and Willmott, M. (2009). Understanding the post-recession consumer. *Harvard Business Review*, 106–112 (July–August).

Ginter, E., Glauser, A., and Richmond, B. O. (1994). Loneliness, social support, and anxiety among two South Pacific cultures. *Psychological Reports*, 74 (3), 875–879.

Goldsmith, R. E., and Clark, R. A. (2012). Materialism, status consumption, and consumer independence. *Journal of Social Psychology*, 152(1), 43–60.

Goodman, J. K., and Irmak, C. (2013). Having versus consuming: Failure to estimate usage frequency makes consumers prefer multi-feature products. *Journal of Marketing Research*, 50(1), 44–54.

Hawkley, L. C. and Cacioppo, J. T. (2010). Loneliness matters: A theoretical and empirical review of consequences and mechanisms. *Annals of Behavioral Medicine*, 40(2), 218–227.

Hombrados-Mendieta, I., García-Martín, M. A., and Gómez-Jacinto, L. (2013). The relationship between social support, loneliness, and subjective well-being in a Spanish sample from a multidimensional perspective. *Social Indicators Research*, 114(3), 1013–1034.

Howell, R. T., and Hill, G. (2009). The mediators of experiential purchases: Determining the impact of psychological needs satisfaction and social comparison. *Journal of Positive Psychology*, 4(6), 511–522.

Hsee, C. K., Yang, Y., Li, N., and Shen, L. (2009). Wealth, warmth, and well-being: Whether happiness is relative or absolute depends on whether it is about money, acquisition, or consumption. *Journal of Marketing Research*, 46(3), 396–409.

Huang, M. H., and Rust, R. T. (2011). Sustainability and consumption. *Journal of the Academy of Marketing Science*, 39(1), 40–54.

Hudders, L., and Pandelaere, M. (2012). The silver lining of materialism: The impact of luxury consumption on subjective well-being. *Journal of Happiness Studies*, 13(3), 411–437.

Kaplan, B. H., Cassel, J. C., and Gore, S. (1977). Social support and health. *Medical Care*, 15(5), 47–58.

Kaplan, S. (2000). New ways to promote pro environmental behavior: Human nature and environmentally responsible behavior. *Journal of Social Issues*, 56(3), 491–508.

Kasser, T. (2002). The Value of Materialism: A Psychological Inquiry. Cambridge, MA: MIT Press.

Kasser, T., Rosenblum, K. L., Sameroff, A. J., Deci, E. L., Niemiec, C. P., Ryan, R. M., . . . and Hawks, S. (2014). Changes in materialism, changes in psychological well-being: Evidence from three longitudinal studies and an intervention experiment. *Motivation and Emotion*, 38(1), 1–22.

Kilbourne, W., and Pickett, G. (2008). How materialism affects environmental beliefs, concern, and environmentally responsible behavior. *Journal of Business Research*, 61(9), 885–893.

La Barbera, P. A., and Gürhan, Z. (1997). The role of materialism, religiosity, and demographics in subjective well-being. *Psychology and Marketing*, 14(1), 71–97.

Lin, N., Dean, A., and Ensel, W. M. (eds). (2013). *Social Support, Life Events, and Depression.* London, UK: Academic Press.

McDonald, S., Oates, C., Thyne, M., Alevizou, P., and McMorland, L.-A. (2009). Comparing sustainable consumption patterns across product sectors. *International Journal of Consumer Studies*, 33, 137–145.

Mellor, D., Stokes, M., Firth, L., Hayashi, Y., and Cummins, R. (2008). Need for belonging, relationship satisfaction, loneliness, and life satisfaction. *Personality and Individual Differences*, 45(3), 213–218.

Mikulincer, M., and Shaver, P. R. (2008). 'Can't buy me love': An attachment perspective on social support and money as psychological buffers. *Psychological Inquiry*, 19(3–4), 167–173.

Nicolao, L., Irwin, J. R., and Goodman, J. K. (2009). Happiness for sale: Do experiential purchases make consumers happier than material. *Journal of Consumer Research*, 36(2), 188–198.

Ottman, J. A., Stafford, E. R., & Hartman, C. L. (2006).Avoiding green marketing myopia: Ways to improve consumer appeal for environmentally preferable products. *Environment*, 48, 22–36.

Pepper, M., Jackson, T., and Uzzell, D. (2009). An examination of the values that motivate socially conscious and frugal consumer behaviors. *International Journal of Consumer Studies*, 33, 126–136.

Pieters, R. (2013). Bidirectional dynamics of materialism and loneliness: Not just a vicious cycle. *Journal of Consumer Research*, 40(4), 615–631.

Richins, M. L. (1994). Special possessions and the expression of material values. *Journal of Consumer Research*, 522–533.

Richins, M. L. (1994). Valuing things: The public and private meanings of possessions. *Journal of Consumer Research*, 21(4), 504–521.

Richins, M. L., and Dawson, S. (1992). A consumer values orientation for materialism and its measurement: Scale development and validation. *Journal of Consumer Research*, 19(3), 303.

Ryan, R. M., Kalil, A., and Leininger, L. (2009). Low-income mothers' private safety nets and children's socio emotional well-being. *Journal of Marriage and Family*, 71(2), 278–297.

Sheth, J. N., Sethia, N. K., and Srinivas, S. (2011). Mindful consumption: A customer-centric approach to sustainability. *Journal of the Academy of Marketing Science*, 39(1), 21–39.

Shwartz, B. (2004). *The Paradox of Choice: Why More Is Less.* New York, NY: Harper Collins.

Tardy, C. H. (1985). Social support measurement. *American Journal of Community Psychology*, 13(2), 187–202.

Thogersen, J., and Crompton, T. (2009). Simple and painless? The limitations of spillover in environmental campaigning. *Journal of Consumer Policy*, 32(2), 141–163.

Tsang, J. A., Carpenter, T. P., Roberts, J. A., Frisch, M. B., and Carlisle, R. D. (2014). Why are materialists less happy? The role of gratitude and need satisfaction in the relationship between materialism and life satisfaction. *Personality and Individual Differences*, 64, 62–66.

Van Boven, L. (2005). Experientialism, materialism, and the pursuit of happiness. *Review of General Psychology*, 9(2), 132.

Van Boven, L., and Gilovich, T. (2003). To do or to have? That is the question. *Journal of Personality and Social Psychology*, 85, 1193–1202.

Watson, D. C. (2014). A model of the materialistic self. *North American Journal of Psychology*, 16(1), 137.

Weinberger, M. F., and Wallendorf, M. (2008). Having vs. doing: Materialism, experientialism, and the experience of materiality. *Advances in Consumer Research*, 35, 257–261.

Weiss, R. S. (1987). Reflections on the present state of loneliness research. *Journal of Social Behavior and Personality*, 2(2), 1.

Young, J. E. (1982). Loneliness, Depression and Cognitive Therapy: Theory and Application. New York, NY: Wiley.

Zhou, X., and Gao, D. G. (2008). Social support and money as pain management mechanisms. *Psychological Inquiry*, 19(3–4), 127–144.

Zimet, G. D., Dahlem, N. W., Zimet, S. G., and Farley, G. K. (1988). The multidimensional scale of perceived social support. *Journal of Personality Assessment*, 52(1), 30–41.

5 Integration of the MLH trap with other aspects of consumer behaviour

5.1 Prior efforts to curb materialism

Recent research has established rising materialism as a negative trend in consumer markets and society that must be dealt with. Most consumers feel pressure to purchase unnecessary products, either due to excessive marketing and advertising or the social lure of status signalling and celebrity diva magnets. The high rate of consumerism is believed to be spreading product discontent and environmental insensitivity (Huang and Rust, 2011; Hurst et al., 2013; Soscia, 2007; Wang and Wallendorf, 2006). Therefore materialism not only renders the consumer socially empty and lonely but emotionally and ethically empty as well.

Several attempts have been made to curb materialism and the rising trend of consumerism, including media campaigns, consumer education schemes and government-regulated consumption policies. There has also been legislation related to children's exposure to advertising and marketing promotions, and several other government interventions in European countries and in the USA. The interventions and counselling are usually aimed at the avoidance of over-buying and at making consumers conscious of the effects of the consumption choices they make.

Amongst the many agencies working on the uphill task of discouraging materialism, two of the most popular are the Adbusters Media Foundation and the Campaign for a Commercial Free Childhood. The Adbusters Media Foundation was founded in 1989. It is a Canadian-based anti-consumerist pro-environment not-for-profit organization. Kalle Lasn and and Bill Schmalz, the founders of the foundation, describe themselves as anti-advertising, and the foundation as a global network of artists, activists, writers, educators and entrepreneurs who want to advance the new social activist movement of the information age. Adbusters has launched numerous international campaigns, including 'Buy Nothing Day' (an international day of protest against consumerism celebrated annually just after Thanksgiving),

'TV Turnoff Week' and 'Occupy Wall Street', and is known for their '*sub-vertisements*', which spoof popular advertisements. They also organize events such as 'credit card cut up', 'zombie walk' and 'whirl mart', aimed at discouraging shopping, especially on credit.

The 'Campaign for a Commercial Free Childhood' was founded in 2000 by Dr Susan Linn, and has built a powerful movement to end the exploitive practice of marketing to children and to promote a modern childhood shaped by what is best for kids, not for corporate profits. The foundation works to reduce marketers' access to children through a variety of tactics and approaches. It supports parents' efforts to raise healthy families by limiting commercial access to children.

Consumer-friendly administrative bodies have also made efforts through taxation and legislation to curb materialistic consumption in different countries. A few financial institutions have taken measures to reduce credit financing to lower the consumption rate via credit cards.

However, the sad reality is that instead of receding, materialism is on the rise in consumer cultures throughout the world. The main reason is that all these media, administrative and legislative interventions focus on the apparent impacts of materialism, and try to break the connection. There are very few efforts to intervene in or control the underlying factors that cause materialism and fuel its impact. Unless these are dealt with, it is difficult to make an effective effort to curb materialism, since such efforts will tackle only the surface issues and not the root factors.

There are various underlying factors that can be regarded as predictors of materialism. These include: the internal psychological factors of the consumer such as self-concept clarity and self-efficacy; external factors such as beliefs about locus of control and level of social self-monitoring; personal traits of the consumer such as greed and envy; social factors faced by the consumer including the religious aspirations, type and level of reference groups, exposure to marketing campaigns; and demographic factors such as age and gender, level of materialistic pursuits and consumption motives. Taken together, it is evident that materialism is a multipronged issue needing a multi-dimensional solution that effectively lowers the negative impacts it has on consumers' lives.

5.2 Establishing a multi-dimensional framework for curbing materialism

A consumer's consumption patterns are largely a product of their own psychological orientations and the surrounding social and environmental factors. These factors fall under different academic disciplines and categories. Of late, materialism has become a widely researched area, under various disciplines. There is a need to sketch a unified materialism theory that acknowledges all these factors and to create effective policies that can help in controlling materialism. The most important factors in both consumers' own lives and the social and environmental arenas that can effectively contribute towards controlling materialism are discussed.

5.2.1 The power of re-socialization through social support

The availability and provision of social support is believed to be of prime importance in resolving many of the social and commercial issues that the consumer of today faces. In this era of intensifying consumerism the plea to completely restrain from material consumption does not seem appropriate. However, an alternative and more applicable approach is to emphasize the 're-socialization' of lifestyle and consumption patterns.

Since social support enhances the perception of being loved, cared for and supported in time of need, it assures the consumer of having individuality or an identity apart from material possessions. So the consumer does not have to rely on material goods to be noticed by others or to signal happiness. The social support provided by the community, social networks and intimate friends leads to increased psychological well-being, lower social loneliness and a higher level of life satisfaction, and plays its characteristic role in sustaining happiness.

Interestingly materialism can play an important part in constructing, maintaining, restoring and transforming social support networks (Hudders and Pandelaere, 2012). There are many things that individuals can possess that can enhance their appeal and make them more 'wanted' and help them fit in with others. Materialism may lead to the restoration of social support by enhancing social acceptance, as it helps to achieve societal goals while promoting significant social relationships.

The key here lies in the employment of materialism as a strategy for strengthening social ties rather than highlighting the individual materialistic agenda. This strategy includes gift giving, social giving, community-building activities and participation in communal development. Therefore, social support can effectively influence the social factors contributing to materialism.

5.2.2 Conscious revamping of the purchase mechanism

The purchase mechanism is the reflection of the consumer's buying behaviour, which is a process that is based on six stages. It starts from the recognition of need, moving on to finding alternatives, evaluating alternatives, making a choice and purchasing, and ends with post-purchase evaluation of the consumption (Solomon et al., 2013). The whole process is influenced by the personal, psychological and social factors surrounding the consumer.

Prior research on materialism has focused only on the psychological factors of the consumer, specifically motives, personality and lifestyle, in determining the buying behaviour and its impacts. However, as the buying behaviour is an amalgam of all three types of factor, there is a need to look beyond the psychological factors and include social and personal factors in order to better evaluate the role and impact of materialism.

To achieve the purpose of an effective purchase process, the consumer needs to consciously review each stage of the consumption process, starting from need recognition. The consumer needs to actively re-evaluate and differentiate between needs and wants. Many a time consumers prefer products that are highly socially desirable, have multiple features and are the new sensation. Such products are usually fairly expensive as compared to less advertised counterparts. The purchase results in temporary excitement and happiness, but soon guilt and product dissatisfaction creep in (Soscia, 2007).

The consumer needs to be conscious of the impact of purchase decisions and focus on things that are really needed rather than just wanted. The content and happiness brought by the consumption can be converted into a long-lasting feeling when consumption motives are realigned. The consumption process may not be beneficial if the consumer does not let go of motives that are relative and symbolic, i.e. the attempt to achieve symbolic benefits through purchases. In contrast, hedonism or necessity-based purchases may provide provisional benefits.

Hedonic or luxury consumption reflects resourcefulness and can improve mood, decrease negativity and increase satisfaction with life through the spillover effect (Deci and Ryan, 2000). However, to make the effect long lasting it needs to be channelized. There is a need for the consumer to identify how and when such consumptions can be made and when to abstain.

While searching for and choosing among alternatives, the consumer should focus upon the available resources, the exact need for the product, the estimated life and usage pattern of the product, and its disposal options. Planned decision-making is not only more useful to the consumer, but it also helps in breaking free of the materialism-loneliness trap.

The whole purchase mechanism and the planned decision-making can effectively impose control over and curb the materialistic orientations of the consumer. There are three ways in which the purchase mechanism and consumer choices can influence materialism: through focusing on socio-centric purchase motivations rather than egocentric purchase motivations, through preferring experiential purchases to material purchases, and through positive self-engrossing product evaluation.

5.2.2.1 Socio-centric purchase motivations

The consumer may undertake three types of discretionary activities when making a purchase. The consumer may make a material purchase or an experiential purchase or may indulge in creative activities to gain satisfaction and happiness. All these activities can be broadly divided into two types of consumption patterns, that is, egocentric purchase patterns and socio-centric purchase patterns.

Egocentric purchase patterns are extrinsically motivated and signify conspicuous buying, creative activities and material purchases for self-gratification. They serve the ego-defensive function, making the consumer feel secure, esteemed and good about themselves (Kardes, Cronley, and Cline, 2010). However, such purchases have a negative impact on happiness as consumers buy joyless material goods that provide comfort but fail to provide pleasure.

On the other hand socio-centric purchase patterns are intrinsically motivated and signify inconspicuous buying, experiential purchases and community activities. Such activities strengthen social relationships, enhance social bonding and provide more opportunities to cherish relationships and improve social skills that can refine and soothe social affiliations.

Socio-centric purchase motivations are centred on sharing and care for others. They nurture a space for thinking about others while making purchase decisions. The consumer needs to understand that purchasing and consumption are not taken in isolation and should reflect on creating a space for sharing the consumption. The impact of socio-centric motivation purchases on the sustained happiness of the consumer remains to be postulated into a theory.

5.2.2.2 Experiential purchases

Experiential purchases are superior to material purchases as they tend to be more resilient to hedonic adaptation, that is, the loss of ability to deliver happiness (positive affect) as time passes. The experiences gained not only provide immediate delight, gratification and psychological nourishment but can be relived, relished and recreated. Many experiences involve difficulties and setbacks that need novel solutions, providing consumers with beneficial learning skills, such as mountaineering, racing and scuba diving. Other experiences such as performing and martial arts require quick wits and stamina, pushing the consumer to more challenges. Experiential purchases have a higher potential for social bonding as they provide opportunities to bring consumers closer to others in real scenarios.

Material purchases, on the other hand, quickly lose their pleasurable aspects due to the fast rate of adaptation, confining the materialistic consumer to a persistent search for more products that can bring that inner satisfaction (Burroughs et al., 2013; Dunn, Gilbert, and Wilson, 2011). Furthermore, Weinberger and Wallendorf (2008) differentiate between material purchases as giving rise to economic capital that can be shared or showed off to others whereas experiential purchases usually give rise to cultural capital that cannot be shared but can be relived and passed on.

When consumption decisions are made, experiential purchases have the tendency to make consumers happier compared to material purchases (Van Boven and Gilovich, 2003). This is because experiences are difficult to compare and evaluate and the happiness acquired is absolute, not relative (Carter and Gilovich, 2010; Hsee et al., 2009). Consumers use maximizing strategy when purchasing material goods and use satisficing strategy when purchasing experiential goods (Carter and Gilovich, 2010; Shwartz, 2004).

Experiential purchases are usually self-defining and wholesome and are made with the intention of deeper experiencing of events and life. Consumers live through experiences with greater chances of social interaction. Most experiential purchases reflect intrinsic motives of self-knowing, understanding, enjoyment and transformation. However, they can sometimes have extrinsic motives as well, especially when the consumer wants to boast of certain experiences or indulge in seeking social desirability (Burroughs et al., 2013). These experiences, such as a leisure trip to the most expensive hotel or watching a play at an expensive theatre, are no better at providing happiness than are most material goods. Thus even experiences with extrinsic motives may not break the materialism trap. The consumer only temporarily enjoys and does not get off the hedonic treadmill, because of the gradual expiration of the boasted-about experience.

Therefore, the major differentiating factor between the different types of experiences and between experiential and material purchases is the level of the engagement of the consumer. The higher the level of engagement with any experience, the greater its ability to create long-lasting happiness and psychological nourishment to be relived, relished and recreated. However different experiences on a continuum of engagement, both physical and mental, offer varying levels of sustained happiness for the consumer, compared to other experiences and material goods, is still an under-researched area (Burroughs et al., 2013).

Moreover, the social dimension of experiential purchases is a factor differentiating them from material purchases. Those experiences that require integration and cooperation from others are more beneficial and substantial to the consumer's happiness compared to those that can be undertaken in isolation. However, there is a lack of research and empirical investigation into how different types of experience help in the getting and sustaining of happiness for the consumer and how exposure and participation in such experiences can be increased.

5.2.2.3 Self-engrossing product evaluation

Prior research on product evaluation generally focuses on the cognitive and affective procedures employed by the consumer in post-purchase evaluation. However, consumer values such as materialism, personality differences and social contexts are seldom researched. It has been discovered that product satisfaction is not only a function of product attributes but the public and social meaning attached to them. Evaluation is also influenced by the materialistic orientations of the consumer. Higher levels of materialism lead to negative product evaluation and a lower level of satisfaction (Wang and Wallendorf, 2006). Product categories with status-signalling potential are preferred by materialists in order to communicate status, but as the feeling wears off with time, dissatisfaction creeps in as the perpetual desire for higher social standing (higher-order goal) is not met. This is because the high price paid for the socially desirable product only pacifies the anxiety temporarily. If at any point in time limited economic resources create a barrier to more purchases, the materialistic consumer is unable to buy the 'next socially desirable product' on the market, which leads to dissatisfaction.

The consumer needs to break the chain of status signalling through acquiring products that are either not required or are already in use. The product must be evaluated on its utilitarian and affective functions and not on symbolic meanings and the consumer should focus on the utilities brought by the product in the daily routine. For this purpose the consumer needs to detach personal identity from the product identity and not rely on the importance of products for self-gratification.

5.2.3 Bridging the MLH gap through social giving

Materialistic orientations render the consumer isolated and confined in their own pursuits. Social ties become weak and unimportant. One way to bridge the gaps created by the materialism-loneliness trap is to voluntarily become involved in social giving. Research suggests that giving to others is positively related to happiness, whereas giving to oneself does not bring any considerable rise in happiness. This is because of the ceiling effect (Burroughs et al., 2013). After a certain level of giving to self, the pleasure such giving ought to give stops. On the other hand the ceiling effect does not come into play in giving to others. Social giving furnishes higher-level fulfilment, a greater sense of efficacy and self-worth, and strengthened social bonding. The greater the level of materialism the higher should be the intent towards charitable giving to mitigate the negative influences (Huang and Rust, 2011).

Materialism signifies self-enhancement values whereas social giving signifies self-transcendence values within the consumer's value system.

Interestingly, materialism and charitable orientations are not mutually exclusive and can co-exist (Mathur, 2013). The consumer needs to develop a systematic schedule of what and when to share with others and a decision as to how to make things better for others along with retaining a personal share of consumption. This tendency to consciously be aware of socio-economic conditions in the surrounding community and make efforts to make a difference weakens the materialistic orientations of the consumer. There is a realization that instead of spending lavishly on the 'self' without acquiring long-lasting happiness, it is better to spend on 'others' and make their happiness a part of personal happiness. Giving to others initiates care and concern for the surrounding community. This strengthens social bonds, creating a form of leverage of social support for the consumer which they cherish, apart from their personal social ties.

Sadly, just as there are materialistic experiences there can be materialistic social giving as well. It is usually aimed at status gains, sexual prospects or a reverse form of conspicuous consumption. The consumer needs to be aware of such motivations as their indulgence will not bring the desired impact of sharing the happiness. Rather the consumer will get stuck deeper in the materialism trap.

The exact nature of giving and the impact of social giving or community development initiatives on the materialistic orientations and happiness gains of the consumer is still an under-researched area.

5.2.4 Substituting the value of materialism with the value of conservation

Materialism is one of the core values that define a consumer's thought patterns. Therefore it cannot be taken out of the system of the consumer's decision-making process. In other words a consumer cannot be fully 'dematerialized'. However, the value of materialism can be substituted with the value of conservation. Conservation is another core value that is in opposition to materialism. If the consumer prioritizes the value of conservation in the decision-making process, the value of materialism can be pushed back.

Conservation is reflected through the consumer attitude of compassion and the taking of proactive steps to preserve and maintain the surrounding systems. As the consumer becomes conscious of the waste of resources, the tendency towards materialistic consumption is lowered. The shift from materialistic orientations can be attained through emphasizing religious and environmental orientations and their role in achieving a higher and sustained level of happiness.

5.2.4.1 Environmentalism

Pro-environment consumer behaviour leads the consumer to actively think about the impact of consumption decisions on the environment. This concern applies to an array of consumer decisions right from the choice of packaging material to the disposal and recycling options available.

Consumers who have a stronger attitude towards recycling show a lower level of materialistic values with positive post-purchase behaviour (Tilikidou and Delistavrou, 2004). High levels of consumerism are most damaging to the environment and create a loss of interest in public life. Pro-environment attitudes and behaviours are negatively associated with materialistic values (Hurst et al., 2013). If there is a resolve towards a sustainable and greener future, consumption patterns should be sensitive to the aspects of environmental impact they create (Huang and Rust, 2011).

Therefore if materialistic orientations are to be restrained it is important for the consumer to learn and understand the impact of consumption decisions. This includes the use of sustainable materials, production procedures, packaging procedures, consumption and disposal and the recycling of used materials. As the consumer becomes conscious of the negative influence that excessive consumption has on the environment there may be a tendency to reduce the consumption level, especially hedonic and conspicuous consumption, i.e. expenditure which is not really required.

Although even the ethical consumer (systematic rational choosers based on advanced environmental information) may behave differently in different product categories, there are certain patterns that are consistent amongst ethical consumers (McDonald et al., 2009). They usually are resistant to wasteful consumption. This suggests that conscious efforts at pro-environmental consumption can impact the level of materialistic orientation in consumers who are sensitive to the environmental influence of their consumption patterns.

5.2.4.2 Religious orientation

Religiosity emphasizes a collective order and system, community service and self-transcendence, which are in opposition to materialistic values. The religiosity level of the consumer moderates the relationship between materialism and subjective well-being (Baker et al., 2013). As materialism and religiosity are in opposition, the higher the level of materialism the higher will be the stress resulting in lower subjective well-being (Swinyard, Kau and Phua, 2002). For a consumer to relieve the stress, it is important to choose amongst the values. As religiosity is a much stronger force and a guiding principle in itself it makes more sense to let go of and control materialistic values.

Moreover, whenever there is a life event that threatens existence (death/ misfortune/threat) the consumer shifts away from materialistic goals. This is specifically true for consumers with high religiosity (Hui et al., 2014). On the other hand fear of death strongly attaches materialistic consumers to brands and their possessions (Rindfleisch, Burroughs, and Wong, 2009). As security remains a major concern with highly materialistic consumers (Clarke and Micken, 2002), only religious faith stresses spirituality and relieves the fear of death and connectivity with material things (Hui et al., 2014; Rindfleisch and Burroughs, 2004).

The consumer's religious belief system can help to realign consumption patterns such that they are directed towards helping others and preserving in the environment the needed faith and conviction. The foremost thing is the consumer's realization and the will to break free from the materialism trap.

5.2.5 Utilizing nostalgia for sustained happiness

Nostalgia and materialism both share the temporal aspect of consumption and therefore have received considerable interest in the field of marketing and advertising over the past few years. Nostalgia can be regarded as powerful memories oriented towards the past that the consumer wants to relive. On the contrary, materialism is focused on fulfilling present needs. Materialistic consumers prefer products high in status and prestige, whereas nostalgic consumers prefer products that relate to past experiences or to people. They may or may not have status or prestige. Nostalgia is negatively related to materialism (Rindfleisch, Freeman, and Burroughs, 2000). Materialism and nostalgia may be oppositional concepts, and marketers employing both appeals for the same product may risk neutralizing the positive effects these two orientations might have individually (Rindfleisch, Freeman, and Burroughs, 2000).

Nostalgia in itself is a positive affect that generates happiness. Moreover it can serve as a repository of affection, widen social connectedness and augment self-worth. Wildschut et al. (2010) found that in addition to being a source of social connectedness, nostalgia increased consumers' perceived capacity to provide emotional support to others.

Nostalgia is an emerging field of research in marketing and consumer behaviour. In recent years, nostalgia is cited as a top trend in products such as toys, food and movies. When people feel nostalgic, social connectedness rises; this heightened desire for social connectedness offsets the desire for money. In effect nostalgia reduces the desire for money and materialistic orientations to have, hold onto and obtain prized valuables. Moreover nostalgia counteracts or reduces loneliness by instilling social connectedness (Zhou et al., 2008). It also increases pro-social behaviour (e.g., helping, volunteering, donating to charity, and decreases anti-social behaviour (e.g., stereotyping) (Lasaleta, Sedikides, and Vohs, 2014). Luxury consumption activities (representing acquisition centrality) such as community care initiatives, family

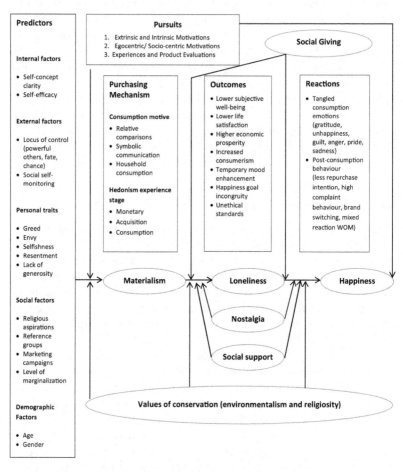

Figure 5.1 Integration of predictors, outcomes, mechanism, consumer reactions,
          mediators and moderators of the materialism trap

picnics, gatherings, birthday parties, vacations, food festivals, home construction and souvenir development may also stimulate nostalgia, which reduces
loneliness and strengthens social relationships. It thus leaves the consumer
feeling happier and more satisfied.

References

Baker, A. M., Moschis, G. P., Ong, F. S., and Pattanapanyasat, R. P. (2013).
    Materialism and life satisfaction: The role of stress and religiosity. *Journal of
    Consumer Affairs*, 47(3), 548–563.

Burroughs, J. E., Chaplin, L. N., Pandelaere, M., Norton, M. I., Ordabayeva, N., Gunz, A., and Dinauer, L. (2013). Using motivation theory to develop a transformative consumer research agenda for reducing materialism in society. *Journal of Public Policy and Marketing*, 32(1), 18–31.

Carter, T. J., and Gilovich, T. (2010). The relative relativity of material and experiential purchases. *Journal of Personality and Social Psychology*, 98(1), 146.

Clarke III, I., and Micken, K. S. (2002). An exploratory cross-cultural analysis of the values of materialism. *Journal of International Consumer Marketing*, 14(4), 65–89.

Deci, E. L., and Ryan, R. M. (2000). The 'what' and 'why' of goal pursuits: Human needs and the self-determination of behavior. *Psychological Inquiry*, 11(4), 227–268.

Dunn, E. W., Gilbert, D. T., and Wilson T. D. (2011). 'If money doesn't make you happy, then you probably aren't spending it right'. *Journal of Consumer Psychology*, 21 (2), 115–125.

Hsee, C. K., Yang, Y., Li, N., and Shen, L. (2009). Wealth, warmth, and well-being: Whether happiness is relative or absolute depends on whether it is about money, acquisition, or consumption. *Journal of Marketing Research*, 46(3), 396–409.

Huang, M. H., and Rust, R. T. (2011). Sustainability and consumption. *Journal of the Academy of Marketing Science*, 39(1), 40–54.

Hudders, L., and Pandelaere, M. (2012). The silver lining of materialism: The impact of luxury consumption on subjective well-being. *Journal of Happiness Studies*, 13(3), 411–437.

Hui, C. H., Chan, S. W., Lau, E. Y., Cheung, S. F., and Mok, D. S. Y. (2014). The role of religion in moderating the impact of life events on material life goals: Some evidence in support of terror management theory. *Mental Health, Religion and Culture*, 17(1), 52–61.

Hurst, M., Dittmar, H., Bond, R., and Kasser, T. (2013). The relationship between materialistic values and environmental attitudes and behaviors: A meta-analysis. *Journal of Environmental Psychology*, 36, 257–269.

Kardes, F. R., Cronley, M. L., and Cline, T. W. (2010). *Consumer Behavior: Science and Practice*. South-Western Cengage Learning.

Lasaleta, J. D., Sedikides, C., and Vohs, K. D. (2014). Nostalgia weakens the desire for money. *Journal of Consumer Research*, 41(3), 713–729.

Mathur, A. (2013). Materialism and charitable giving: Can they co-exist? *Journal of Consumer Behaviour*, 12(3), 149–158.

McDonald, S., Oates, C., Thyne, M., Alevizou, P., and McMorland, L.-A. (2009). Comparing sustainable consumption patterns across product sectors. *International Journal of Consumer Studies*, 33, 137–145.

Rindfleisch, A., and Burroughs, J. E. (2004). Terrifying thoughts, terrible materialism? Contemplations on a terror management account of materialism and consumer behavior. *Journal of Consumer Psychology*, 14(3), 219–224.

Rindfleisch, A., Burroughs, J. E., and Wong, N. (2009). The safety of objects: Materialism, existential insecurity, and brand connection. *Journal of Consumer Research*, 36(1), 1–16.

Rindfleisch, A., Freeman, D., and Burroughs, J. E. (2000). Nostalgia, materialism, and product preference: An initial inquiry. *Advances in Consumer Research*, 27, 36–41.

Shwartz, B. (2004). *The Paradox of Choice: Why More Is Less.* New York, NY: Harper Collins.

Solomon, M. R., Baboosy, G. J., Askegaard S. T., and Hogg, M. K. (2013). *Consumer Behavior: A European Perspective.* 5th edition. Harlow, UK: Pearson.

Soscia, I. (2007). Gratitude, delight, or guilt: The role of consumers' emotions in predicting post-consumption behaviours. *Psychology and Marketing,* 24(10), 871–894.

Swinyard, W. R., Kau, A. K., and Phua, H. Y. (2002). A meta-analysis of the relationships between happiness, materialism and spirituality in the US and Singapore. *Asia Pacific Advances in Consumer Research,* 5, 246–247.

Tilikidou, I., and Delistavrou, A. (2004). The influence of the materialistic values on consumers' pro-environmental post-purchase behavior. In *Marketing Theory and Applications, Proceedings of the 2004 American Marketing Association Winter Educators' Conference,* 15, 42–49.

Van Boven, L., and Gilovich, T. (2003). To do or to have? That is the question. *Journal of Personality and Social Psychology,* 85, 1193–1202.

Wang, J., and Wallendorf, M. (2006). Materialism, status signaling, and product satisfaction. *Journal of the Academy of Marketing Science,* 34(4), 494–505.

Weinberger, M. F., and Wallendorf, M. (2008). Having vs. doing: Materialism, experientialism, and the experience of materiality. *Advances in Consumer Research,* 35, 257–261.

Wildschut, T., Sedikides, C., Routledge, C., Arndt, J., and Cordaro, F. (2010). Nostalgia as a repository of social connectedness: The role of attachment-related avoidance. *Journal of Personality and Social Psychology,* 98(4), 573–578.

Zhou, X., Sedikides, C., Wildschut, T., and Gao, D. G. (2008). Counteracting loneliness on the restorative function of nostalgia. *Psychological Science,* 19(10), 1023–1029.

6 Socio-psychological theory of the MLH trap

6.1 Why the MLH trap exists

A consumer gets caught up in the materialism-loneliness-unhappiness trap when they utilize material possessions as a proxy measure for success and happiness. The consumer purchases endlessly in an attempt to buy happiness. In effect the materialistic purchases provide only temporary happiness, but give rise to loneliness as well. The failure to achieve success or happiness creates a void in the consumer's life. Again the consumer attempts to fill this void through indulging in more materialistic consumption and remains unsuccessful. This is because they have already disturbed the social network and have lower prospects for social sharing, resulting in greater loneliness. The lonely consumer indulges in more materialism to shake-off the feeling, leading to greater unhappiness. The consumer as a result is unable to break free of the cyclical trap. Materialism and loneliness share a bidirectional, positive relationship, whereas the relationship between loneliness and happiness is negative.

Although the trap has been established theoretically, concrete efforts to provide a theoretical understanding of how the consumer can break free of it have yet not transpired. The existing research remains inadequate in furnishing contingencies that make the phenomenon directly researchable. The materialism literature remains fragmented under different disciplines and subjects that study the consumer's life from various social, psychological, cultural and media-communicational standpoints. Unfortunately, a unified materialism theory in relation to consumer happiness has not yet crystallized.

It is important to devise a solution to untangle the trap as the unhappiness caused by materialistic purchases results in continuous brand/product switching, undesirable post-purchase evaluations and shifting brand loyalties, which is a concern for both theorists and marketers alike.

6.1.1 Three main constructs

In order to advance the theory of the materialism trap it is important to understand the mental configuration of the three main constructs of the trap, i.e., materialism, loneliness and happiness. These have been discussed in earlier sections of the book. The following is a quick recap of the definitions of the main constructs that develop the trap:

Materialism is 'craving for worldly possessions as a steering value of life that ensures happiness and success in a materialist's belief.' It has *three aspects*, namely centrality (major goal in life is acquiring worldly possession), happiness (quest for material goods is the primary source of satisfaction), and success (worldly possessions act as an indicator of success to others) (Richins and Dawson, 1992). It is the consumer's tendency to enhance self-esteem, prestige and self-worth through possessing goods and prized valuables.

Loneliness is a relatively persistent experience of emotional suffering caused by rejection or exclusion by others from a social group, being misunderstood and alienated, or lacking suitable and desirable social partners for various activities, specifically the events that furnish prospects for intimacy and a sense of communal integration (Rook, 1984).

Happiness is a state of mind that results from being eudemonically and hedonically satisfied. It is composed of positive affect, absence of negative affect and satisfaction with life as a whole (Fave et al., 2011).

6.1.2 Socio-psychological factors

Several socio-psychological factors have been identified as directly impacting materialism, loneliness and happiness, independently as well as contingently to the materialism-loneliness-unhappiness trap. The eight factors that have been identified have the capacity to comprehensively unfold the trap.

Three of these factors reflect psychological personal motivations of the consumer pertaining to their purchase mechanism, namely *ego-centric* and *socio-centric motivations, experiential purchases* and self-engrossing *product evaluation*. The fourth factor is *social support*, which reflects the social setup of the consumer. The next three factors, *religiosity, environmentalism* and *social giving*, reveal socio-cultural identities. Finally, *nostalgia* represents the socio-psychological processes of the consumer.

Sections 6.3 to 6.5 discuss the impact of these socio-psychological factors, firstly on materialism, then on loneliness and then on happiness, and, finally, as contingency factors to the materialism-loneliness/loneliness-happiness relationships.

6.2 Socio-psychological theory of the materialism trap

Whenever the consumer utilizes material possessions as a proxy measure of success and happiness in an attempt for self-gratification and self-enhancement, they substitute material goods for relationships and become a victim of loneliness and happiness. As described above, this is academically known as the materialism-loneliness-happiness (MLH) trap. It is increasingly becoming imperative to find a solution to this trap as the lack of happiness leads to continuous brand/product switching, undesirable post-purchase evaluations and shifting brand loyalties. There are several social, cultural, psychological and demographic factors that give rise to the MLH trap. The purpose of the theory is to suggest ways to understand the trap and predict how the trap can be untangled.

The theory argues that controlling materialism means nipping the evil in the bud, i.e., saving consumers from being captured in the trap. Materialism can be reduced by bringing about a change in the *purchase mechanism (i.e., purchase motivations, experiential purchase and product evaluation)* and shifting the reliance on material goods to *social giving, environmentalism* and *religiosity*. This theory further introduces five boundary conditions that can decrease the flows in the MLH trap, i.e., from materialism towards loneliness and then from loneliness to unhappiness. Specifically, the theory suggests that the strength of the materialism-loneliness relationship can be weakened through the provision of the *social support, nostalgia, social giving, environmentalism* and *religiosity*. Two of these contingent factors – social support and nostalgia – can also mitigate the loneliness-happiness path. Overall, all of the eight factors (italicized above) can help sustain the happiness of consumers. The following paragraphs elaborate these factors' relevance in understanding the MLH trap.

Reduction in materialism can be achieved by bringing about a change in the purchase mechanism in three ways. The *first* is by focusing on socio-centric purchase motivations rather than egocentric; which have a positive relationship with materialism and enhance it. Whereas Socio-centric motivations have a negative relationship with materialism and curb it. They strengthen social relationships and improve social skills that can refine and soothe affiliations. *Secondly*, experiential purchases provide satisfaction, delight and long-lasting psychological nourishment. These are resilient to hedonic adaptation and give rise to cultural capital that can be relived and passed on. The satisfaction acquired is absolute, not relative, making it ideal for combating materialism. The relationship is thus negative. *Thirdly*, product evaluation on utilitarian and affective functions of the product and a detachment from the symbolic meaning of the product, i.e., its potential to signal status, leads to a reduction in materialism, signifying a negative relationship.

Moreover, materialism can also be curbed through enhanced environmentalism, which has a negative relationship with materialism. It motivates a shift away from wasteful consumption patterns while encouraging sustainable consumption. Religiosity also helps in controlling materialistic desires. It realigns consumption patterns, directing them towards helping others, and preserves the milieu with the faith and conviction needed to lower materialistic orientations.

The link between materialism and loneliness can be weakened through social giving, nostalgia and the provision of social support. Social giving can be used as a channelizing medium for materialism and loneliness. It has a negative relationship with materialism and can bridge the isolation created. Similarly, nostalgia can serve as a repository of affection, widen social connectedness and augment self-worth. It counters materialism through powerful memories of past experiences and people. It highlights the personal preciousness that subdues the prestige and status factors attached to the product, offsetting materialism with desire for social connectivity. It increases pro-social behaviour and decreases anti-social behaviour. Social support also helps in reducing the anxieties and general insecurities of the consumer which are the forerunner of materialism and reduces loneliness by providing more interaction opportunities.

Environmentalism and religiosity also help in weakening the link between materialism and loneliness. Environmentalism is a motivational booster that reduces the materialistic drive while bringing consumers closer to those who have similar beliefs, enhancing connectivity. It thus weakens the relationship. Similarly religiosity provides a greater level of connectivity with surroundings and people, shifting the consumer towards self-transcendence and system conservation. It instils a sense of care for the people around, lowering both materialism and loneliness.

Happiness can be enhanced through revamping the purchase mechanism; enhancing social giving, environmentalism, religiosity and nostalgia; and the provision of social support. Socio-centric motivations refine and soothe social affiliations, setting the foundation for sustained happiness, whereas the more engaging and intrinsic experiential purchases are, the higher is their capability to provide sustained happiness. Dissatisfaction with the purchase process can be controlled by detachment from the symbolic meaning of the purchase and its evaluation on a utilitarian basis. Social giving can provide internal satisfaction and soulful nourishment leading to sustained happiness. Environmentalism instils a sense of purpose, care and accomplishment that fulfils higher-order needs that play their characteristic role in sustained happiness. Religiosity provides a sense of spiritual accomplishment that fulfils higher order needs. The satisfaction engendered by community care and being instrumental in system preservation enhances happiness and sustains it at a greater level. Nostalgia revitalizes the positive affect of the consumer. They feel relaxed and comfortable remembering good times from the past, which results in enhanced happiness. Social support lessens the feeling of isolation and enhances the prospects for the sharing of that help and bridges the gap between loneliness and happiness.

6.3 Impact of socio-psychological factors on materialism

The socio-psychological factors that impact materialism are egocentric purchase motivations, socio-centric purchase motivations, experiential purchases, product evaluation, environmentalism and religiosity. These are now discussed in detail.

6.3.1 Impact of purchase mechanism on materialism

The purchase mechanism includes egocentric and socio-centric purchase motivations, experiential purchases and product evaluation. The foremost factor in untangling the trap is the purchase mechanism, which represents the personal psychological factors of the consumer. Any change in consumption patterns can bring about a change in materialism; this requires a realignment of consumption motives and the purchase mechanism. There are three ways to influence the whole process. It can be achieved through focusing on socio-centric purchase motivations instead of egocentric motivations, indulging in experiential purchases and pursuing positive non-self-engrossing product evaluation.

6.3.1.1 Egocentric purchase motivations and materialism

Egocentric purchase motivations are centred towards *self-gratification* and desire to elaborate personality through material goods. They reflect possession-defined success and the acquisition-as-the-pursuit-of-happiness facet of materialism. The purchase decision is motivated by self-enhancement aspirations. The consumer with egocentric purchase motivations utilizes material goods as a status signal or as a proxy measure of happiness. The expectation is never fulfilled and eventually despair, hostility and loneliness fill the void created by this substitution. Therefore even with high levels of consumption, the materialistic pursuits are not fulfilling, as there is no end to the objective of gratification through material goods; this signifies the materialism trap. The consumer keeps on consuming more, fuelled by ego-centric motivations. The essence is captured in the following proposition.

P_{1a}: *Enhancement in egocentric purchase motivations increases the materialism of the consumer*

6.3.1.2 Socio-centric purchase motivations and materialism

Socio-centric purchase motivations are centred on sharing and care for others. They nurture a space for thinking about others while making purchase decisions. However, such motivations do not generate automatically and different consumers exhibit different levels of socio-centric motivations, reflecting the psychological build-up inherent in the consumer.

To enhance the level of such motivations it is important that the consumer is inspired, encouraged and trained to think about others while making purchases. This can be achieved through the promotion and highlighting of the philanthropic efforts of various celebrated individuals and organizations and the impact of such efforts on the industry and consumers. Moreover highlighting and educating regarding the impacts of product use/overuse and disposal may also help in the training of consumers and in encouraging them towards sharing and thoughtful usage. The impact of socio-centric purchase motivations on materialism still needs to be postulated into a theory. The following proposition is suggested.

P_{1b}: *Enhancement in socio-centric purchase motivations decreases the materialism of the consumer*

6.3.1.3 Experiential purchases and materialism

Experiential purchases are the 'purchasing of products of experiences' in the form of social memories, tools of social protection, connection, events, activities or social production. They usually are self-defining and wholesome and are made with the intention of deeper experiencing of events and life. Such experiential purchases, which reflect intrinsic motives, self-knowing and understanding, transformation agendas and a higher level of engagement, have a greater ability to furnish psychological nourishment. Moreover, the social dimension of experiential purchases differentiates them from material purchases, requiring integration and cooperation from others, thus being more beneficial to the consumer's satisfaction level. However, as discussed earlier materialistic experiences with extrinsic motives do not provide the same benefits; rather they approximate material purchases. Experiential purchases that are intrinsically motivated and engaging loosen the consumer's emphasis on materialism as a way of gratification and pleasure seeking. Such experiences not only provide immediate delight, gratification and psychological nourishment but can be relived, relished and recreated. The discussion leads to the following proposition.

P_{1c}: *A higher number of intrinsic engaging experiential purchases lowers the materialism of the consumer*

6.3.1.4 Product evaluation and materialism

Product satisfaction is a function of product attributes, along with the public and social meaning attached to the product and the level of the consumer's materialistic orientations. Product dissatisfaction often creeps in during evaluation, not because of the product's attributes but whenever the consumer cannot fulfil the perpetual desire for higher social standing and status signalling through that product. The consumer's materialistic anxiety is only temporarily pacified by the materialistic purchase and they soon realize that the high price paid for the socially desirable product is no longer communicated. Limited economic resources may create a barrier to buying more socially desirable products in the market, which not only leads to dissatisfaction but to a continuous focus on acquiring more.

The consumer needs to break the chain of signalling status via acquiring products that are either not required or that are already in use. For this purpose they need to detach personal identity from the product identity and not rely on the importance given to products for self-gratification. The essence of the discussion is given in the following proposition.

P_{1d}:*A greater level of non-self-engrossment in product evaluation decreases materialism*

6.3.2 Impact of environmentalism on materialism

Environmentalism is the practice of consuming less products or recycled products, compromising on price, convenience, brand and performance, to highlight environmental sustainability concerns and principles (Pepper et al., 2009). The value of materialism crystallizes as a negative tendency when it exceeds other values of the value system of a consumer. One way to untangle the materialism trap is to highlight and consciously make efforts to enhance and adopt at a practical level values that are in opposition to materialism. Environmentalism represents the value of conservation and is negatively associated with materialistic values. It can actively encourage the consumer to shift away from wasteful consumption. Environmentalism helps the consumer to realize the obnoxious effects unwanted material consumption may have on the environment and the economic system. The following proposition summarizes the discussion.

P_{1e}: *An increase in the level of active environmentalism lowers the level of materialism*

6.3.3 Impact of religiosity on materialism

Religiosity is the level of influence of religion on the philosophy and principles of a consumer's life, daily activities, praying schedules and ways, religious services and routine (Wilkes et al., 1986). The consumer's religious belief system can help to realign consumption patterns such that they are directed towards helping others and preserving the milieu of faith and conviction. The consumer's realization is integral to creating the will to break free from the materialism trap. Religiosity emphasizes a collective order and system, community service and self-transcendence, which are in opposition to materialistic values. A higher level of religiosity shifts the consumer's emphasis from material purchase for oneself to various forms of giving to others. The shift is associated with greater faith in the divine and accompanied by greater gratitude and appreciation of all the material possession already used by the consumer. In simpler terms, religiosity reduces the drive for more valuables and substitutes it with appreciation.

P_{1f}: *An increase in the level of religiosity lowers the level of materialism*

6.4 Impact of socio-psychological factors on loneliness

Loneliness itself is a sociological issue and is greatly impacted by the socio-psychological factors surrounding the consumer. However, loneliness is a mere perception and is relative to the conditions the consumer lives in. Therefore, a change in the satisfaction level achieved from the consumption process or the removal of the ills of materialism automatically alters the level of perception of loneliness. The factors identified concerning the consumer that impact loneliness are nostalgia and social giving. These are discussed further below.

6.4.1 Impact of nostalgia on loneliness

Nostalgia is a sentimental longing for the past and memories accompanied by pleasure and sadness. It is a prevalent experience, and draws on uniquely human cognitive abilities (Wildschut et al., 2010).

Nostalgia is fast becoming a distinct area of research. It also contributes towards the materialism theory. Nostalgia reduces loneliness by instilling social connectedness, increasing pro-social behaviour (e.g., helping, volunteering, donating to charity) and decreasing anti-social behaviour (e.g., stereotyping). Nostalgia helps in remembering important points and people in the past, which enhances the desire to relive and reconnect, thus acting as a stimulus towards social connectivity. Nostalgia also keeps relationships emotionally refreshed without physical interaction. Loneliness has been discussed in Chapter 3, and defined as a perception of being alone. It may or may not be accompanied by actual isolation of the consumer. Some part of loneliness is developed in the consumer's thinking and is not factual. Therefore any contrasting and counteracting thinking pattern may help against loneliness syndrome. The discussion in summarized in the following proposition.

P_{2a}: *Nostalgia lowers the level of perception of loneliness*

6.4.2 Impact of social giving on loneliness

Giving to others initiates care and concern that strengthens social bonds. Social giving is the practice of being benevolent, giving and sharing with others (BarTal, 1976). It is a form of positive social behaviour. The practice of social giving enhances the consumer's sensitivity to the surrounding environment and people and develops the tendency to be more receptive to the needs of others. It can help to reduce the anxiety created by the feeling of being alone or not being a part of something important. Social giving can be a public and group activity as well, which provides the consumer with more interaction opportunities. Moreover it can be a means towards enhancing the social support network. The following proposition makes the argument.

P_{2b}: *Investing in social giving lowers the loneliness level of the consumer*

6.5 Impact of socio-psychological factors on happiness

The socio-psychological factors impact happiness in the same way as they impact materialism. The factors that have been identified as having an impact on happiness are: egocentric and socio-centric purchase motivations, experiential purchases, product evaluation, environmentalism and religiosity, social giving and nostalgia. An important consideration in discussing these contingencies is that happiness can be gained through several activities, but usually it is fleeting and often accompanied by later negative feelings. The contingencies that are discussed here are those that have comparatively longer lasting and sustained impact on the consumer's happiness. These are now discussed in detail.

6.5.1 Impact of purchase mechanism on happiness

Changes in consumption motives and the purchase mechanism can be instrumental in achieving a sustained level of happiness. This can be achieved through focusing on socio-centric purchase motivations rather than egocentric motivations, indulging in experiential purchases and pursuing positive self-engrossing product evaluation.

6.5.1.1 Egocentric purchase motivations and happiness

While pursuing egocentric purchase motivations the unending desire to promote self through material goods pushes the consumer towards loneliness and anxiety. The purchases only provide temporary happiness. Soon the realization that the purpose is not effectively fulfilled pushes sadness and despair back into the consumer's life. The consumer lacks sharing prospects due to the egoistic self-centred purchases; therefore the contentment of purchase is never translated into sustained happiness. Egocentric purchases have almost the same impact on the whole purchase cycle as materialism itself. This is the major loophole in the purchase cycle, which should be avoided. If purchases are made only for self-enhancement and glorification, the purchase process remains fragmented and lacks soul. The satisfaction it brings is temporary and there begins the whole cycle of materialism once again. Egocentric purchases reflect the second facet of materialism, i.e., acquisition for the pursuit of happiness. The discussion is encapsulated in the following proposition.

P_{3a}: *Enhancement of egocentric purchase motivations increases happiness but it is only temporary*

6.5.1.2 Socio-centric purchase motivations and happiness

Socio-centric purchase motivations highlight the fact that purchasing and consumption are not undertaken in isolation and the consumer should reflect upon creating a space for sharing the consumption with others. The sharing prospect enhances opportunities for reaping extended benefits from the purchase and its usage. The third facet of materialism, i.e., acquisition centrality, arises out of intrinsic goal motivations, reflecting socio-centric purchase motivations. Hedonic consumption or acquisition centrality provides consumers with control and autonomy without any extrinsic or ulterior motives that bring happiness. The consumer needs to make conscious efforts to emphasize the facet of acquisition centrality, that is, detaching the product, its use and evaluation from the social and symbolic meanings reflected in possession of it. Acquisition centrality can be enhanced only through changes in the way purchases are made and products are utilized, such that they could be used to strengthen the support networks of the consumer. Increased socio-centric purchase motivations increase the tendency to share and achieve a higher level of satisfaction from purchases. The argument is summarized in the following proposition.

P_{3b}: *Enhancement in socio-centric purchase motivations increases sustained happiness of the consumer*

6.5.1.3 Experiential purchases and happiness

Experiential purchases have a greater potential to provide happiness to the consumer. However, a consumer cannot engage in experiential purchases at all times, as there is a need for non-experiential purchases as well. So, in order to break free from the trap and relish sustained happiness over a longer period of time, the consumer needs to focus on spending to a predefined planned pattern on both needed material purchases and experiential purchases, striking a balance between the two. However, there is a lack of research and empirical investigation into how different types of experience help in obtaining and sustaining happiness for the consumer and how exposure to and participation in such experiences can be increased. Moreover how different experiences on a continuum of engagement offer varying levels of sustained happiness for the consumer is still an under researched area.

Experiential purchases have higher potential for social bonding as they provide opportunities to bring consumers closer in real scenarios, giving rise to cultural capital that can be relived and passed on. Experiential purchases tend to make consumers happier as compared to material purchases, as they are difficult to compare and evaluate and the happiness acquired is absolute, not relative. Experiential purchases are usually self-defining, wholesome and made with the intention of deeper experiencing of life. The higher the level of engagement of any experience, the greater is its ability to furnish long-lasting happiness and psychological nourishment, and to be relived, relished and recreated. Moreover due to the social dimension of experiential purchases they require integration and cooperation from others and are more beneficial and substantial to the consumer's happiness.

P_{3c}: *A higher number of intrinsic engaging experiential purchases increases the level of sustained happiness*

6.5.1.4 Product evaluation and happiness

Product evaluation is the consumer's assessment of the satisfaction achieved by the use of a product. When the product is evaluated on its utilitarian and affective functions and not on its symbolic meanings, the consumer can benefit from it in the intended way and dissatisfaction is reduced. Therefore, a decrease in product dissatisfaction can lead to an enhanced level of happiness. Moreover when the consumer focuses on the utilities brought by the product in the daily routine and not on ulterior purposes, they do not proportion happiness to product use. The proposition highlights that reliance should not be placed on engrossment for product evaluation.

P_{3d}: *A greater level of non-self-engrossment in product evaluation increases happiness*

6.5.2 Impact of environmentalism and religiosity on happiness

Both environmentalism and religiosity provide the consumer with a sense of purpose and accomplishment in life that fulfils the higher-order needs. The satisfaction attached to taking care of the environment and playing a role in its preservation enhances happiness and sustains it at a greater level. Moreover religiosity strengthens the belief that such preservation is the right way to follow, increasing the satisfaction arising even from lower volumes of and cheaper consumption. Thus the following proposition:

P_{3e}: *An increase in environmentalism and religiosity enhances the level of sustained happiness*

6.5.3 Impact of social giving on happiness

Social giving provides higher-level fulfilment, a greater sense of efficacy and self-worth and strengthened social bonding. Giving to others enhances subjective well-being and happiness. A sense of purpose associated with social giving brings personal satisfaction to consumers, thus contributing to happiness. The continuation of the practice of social giving has the potential to provide sustained happiness over a period of time. The exact nature of giving and the impact of social giving or community development initiatives on the happiness gains of the consumer is still an under-researched area. The following proposition reflects the discussion.

P_{3f}: *Investing in social giving increases the level of sustained happiness*

6.5.4 Impact of nostalgia on happiness

Nostalgia brings with it strong and powerful memories that can become a source of happiness for consumers. Happiness is a product of positive affect, the absence of negative affect and satisfaction with life. Nostalgia plays an important role in revitalizing the positive affect of the consumer. The consumer feels relaxed and comfortable in remembering good times from the past. Nostalgia is also sometimes utilized as a supporting mechanism, especially in times of isolation, to instil a feeling of being cherished, loved and remembered. Similarly, nostalgia can be helpful in bringing back good memories of things/valuables used in the past, along with sentiments of how they gave pleasure previously.

P_{3g}: *Nostalgia increases the level of sustained happiness*

6.6 Contingency factors for the M-L relationship

Socio-psychological factors not only impact materialism, loneliness and happiness separately but also act as contingency factors to the relationship between materialism and loneliness. The most important factor, which can play a critical role in mitigating the M-L relationship, is the provision of social support. Social support is one of the major factors that is not directly within the control of the consumer; instead, it is the social setup surrounding the consumer. However, the personal behaviour of the consumer does impact the continued provision of social support. This is because social support already available maybe strengthened or damaged due to the personal social behaviour of the consumer. Therefore, the availability and provision of social support are a given for the consumer's circumstances, whereas the continuation of social support is dependent on an amalgam of factors based on the consumer's social behaviour. The other contingency factors that impact the materialism-loneliness relationship are environment, religiosity and social giving. These are discussed next.

6.6.1 Impact of social support on the M-L relationship

Social support is the amalgam of factors that create the perception that one is cared for, will receive help and assistance from others and is a participant in a supportive social network (Kaplan et al., 1977). It has four properties namely, *content* (meanings given to the relationships), *directedness* (relationships and their reciprocity), *intensity* (level of binding and obligation) and *frequency* (level of interactions).

The availability and provision of social support is believed to be of prime importance in resolving many of the social and commercial issues faced by a consumer. Social support enhances the perception of being loved, cared for and supported in time of need. It therefore provides the consumer with individuality or an identity separate from the material possessions and status signals. Social support lessens the general insecurities of a materialistic consumer and reduces the anxiety and despair arising out of loneliness. Thus it can play a major role in loosening the materialism-loneliness trap. It reduces the emphasis on materialistic purchases for acquiring social status, desirability and fame. The following proposition summarizes the discussion.

P_{4a}: *Increased provision of social support lowers the need for materialism as a substitute for loneliness, thus weakening the M-L relationship*

6.6.2 Impact of environmentalism and religiosity on the M-L relationship

Environmentalism enhances sharing prospects and instils a sense of care for the environment and the people around. It not only lowers the motivation of materialism as a self-enhancement tool but also allows connection to others with similar beliefs, giving rise to a 'social family.' Moreover religiosity enhances faith and beliefs resulting in lesser reliance on materialism for pleasure and gratification and a greater sense of obligation towards others. Both environmentalism and religiosity represent self-transcendence values and oppose the value of materialism, signifying the importance of social ties in society. Environmentalism reduces the attraction of new, shimmering or prestigious buying. It enhances the consumer's focus on recycling and reimagining new ways to use the products already bought, for a longer period of time, such that waste is minimal. Similarly religiosity focuses on the goodness of things already acquired. The blessings which the consumer enjoys are a privilege that they should be thankful for, cherish and share with others. Religiosity highlights the importance of sharing the goodness with others rather than focusing on self-enhancement or enrichment. The essence is captured in the following propositions.

P_{4b}: *An increase in environmentalism and religiosity weakens the link between materialism and loneliness*

6.6.3 Impact of social giving on M-L relationship

Materialism renders the consumer isolated and confined in their own pursuits. Social ties become weak and unimportant. Relationships are few and are often materialistically overshadowed. Involvement in social giving can bridge the isolation created by materialism and can reduce loneliness levels. Social giving also implies self-transcendence values, like environmentalism and religiosity. However, social giving is different from both environmentalism and religiosity in relation to reducing materialism. Social giving is not in opposition to materialism, as are religiosity or environmentalism (which shun excessive consumption); rather it indirectly reduces the need for gratification through material possession. At the same time it also increases the social network of the consumer, through their engagement in social giving activities, and connections with those who are affected by it. This tendency towards understanding socio-economic conditions and helping the surrounding community not only weakens the desire for materialistic pursuits, but also establishes stronger social links. So even if the consumer is pursuing materialistic purchases, social giving does not lead towards loneliness as there is a larger social network to rely on. Therefore social giving is a stronger anchor for the 'new materialism', where materialism is the accepted norm, but with modifications (Simms and Potts, 2012). The discussion is reflected in the following proposition.

P_{4c}: *Investing in social giving lowers the need for gratification through materialism while widening the social network, which weakens the M-L relationship*

6.6.4 Impact of nostalgia on the M-L relationship

Nostalgia and materialism both share the temporal aspects of consumption and are in opposition to each other. Nostalgia is negatively related to materialism but in itself has a positive affect that generates happiness. Nostalgia can also play a role in lowering materialistic orientations as it can serve as a repository for affection, widen social connectedness and augment self-worth. Nostalgia can counter present materialistic needs for status and prestige through powerful memories of past experiences and people, making the consumer want to relive these. The use of nostalgic appeals highlights personal preciousness for the consumer that subdues the prestige and status factors of the product. When people feel nostalgic the desire for social connectedness rises, which offsets the desire for money. In effect it reduces the desire to have, hold and obtain prized valuables, while increasing the desire to relive memories and be with cherished ones. The following proposition reflects the discussion.

P_{4d}: *Nostalgia offsets materialism by enhancing desire for social connectivity*

6.7 Contingency factors for the L-H relationship

Social support has been identified as the most important factor, and it can play a critical role in mitigating the L-H relationship. It is discussed as follows.

6.7.1 Impact of social support on the L-H relationship

Social support provides the basis for a sustained level of happiness. It leads to increased psychological well-being, lower social loneliness and a higher level of life satisfaction, and plays its characteristic role in sustained happiness. It increases sharing prospects for the consumer and the consumer feels happier to share and cherish even a lesser amount of goods. Social support helps in fighting the root causes of loneliness, i.e., the perception of being left alone. At the same time the prospect of being a part of a larger group can initiate a feeling of relativeness. It thus provides a feel good factor over a period of time. The proposition is as follows.

P_{5a}: *Increased provision of social support increases sharing prospects which lower loneliness and enhance happiness*

6.7.2 Impact of nostalgia on the L-H relationship

Nostalgia increases the perception of connectivity without physical objectivity and can play its characteristic role in weakening the relationship between loneliness and happiness. Since loneliness is not an actual absence of social company and connectivity, rather a perception of the consumer that they have no one to share and communicate with, nostalgia offsets this feeling because it is also based on the perception of connectivity and being closer to someone or some event in the past. As discussed earlier nostalgia enhances positive mood emotions, and can help in bridging the loneliness-unhappiness gap.

P$_{5b}$: *Nostalgia increases the perception of connectivity, which lowers loneliness and enhances happiness*

6.8 Summary

The integrated model of the materialism-loneliness-happiness (MLH) trap identified the constructs that are significant to the untangling of the trap. The theoretical advancement establishes the importance of each of the constructs in untangling the trap by forming the proposed relationships among the constructs and their direction. The proposed integrated model (Figure 6.1) rests upon the established relationships between the three main variables, i.e., materialism, loneliness and happiness, and the impact of socio-psychological factors upon these.

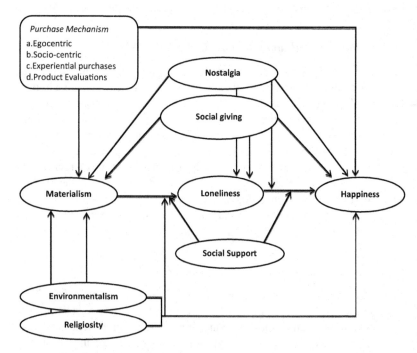

Figure 6.1 Unfolding the MLH trap: Impact of socio-psychological factors on the materialism-loneliness-happiness trap

References

BarTal, D. (1976). *Prosocial Behaviour: Theory and Research.* Washington, DC: Hemisphere Publishing Corporation.

Fave, D. A., Brdar, I., Freire, T., Vella, B. D., and Wissing, M. P. (2011). The eudaimonic and hedonic components of happiness: Qualitative and quantitative findings. *Social Indicators Research*, 100(2), 185–207.

Kaplan, B. H., Cassel, J. C., and Gore, S. (1977). Social support and health. *Medical Care*, 15(5), 47–58.

Pepper, M., Jackson, T., and Uzzell, D. (2009). An examination of the values that motivate socially conscious and frugal consumer behaviours. *International Journal of Consumer Studies*, 33, 126–136.

Richins, M. L., and Dawson, S. (1992). A consumer values orientation for materialism and its measurement: Scale development and validation. *Journal of Consumer Research*, 19(3), 303.

Rook, K. S. (1984). Promoting social bonding: Strategies for helping the lonely and socially isolated. *American Psychologist*, 39(12), 1398–1407.

Simms, A., & Potts, R. (2012). *The New Materialism.* London, UK: bread, print & roses.

Wildschut, T., Sedikides, C., Routledge, C., Arndt, J., and Cordaro, F. (2010). Nostalgia as a repository of social connectedness: The role of attachment-related avoidance. *Journal of Personality and Social Psychology*, 98(4), 573–578.

Wilkes, R. E., Burnett, J. J., and Howell, R. D. (1986). On the meaning and measurement of religiosity in consumer research. *Journal of the Academy of Marketing Science*, 14(1), 47–56.

7 Discussion and conclusion

7.1 Discussion on integration

In the current era of globalization and consumerism, materialism has been realized as a universal, prevailing consumer value that shapes consumers' consumption choices to a large degree. Materialism is the consumer's tendency to enhance self-esteem, prestige and self-worth through possessing goods and prized valuables. An excessive emphasis on acquiring and showing off such valuables is disruptive to the consumer's social affiliations and subjective well-being, resulting in loneliness, despair and unhappiness. This materialism-loneliness-unhappiness trap becomes visible and vicious when the consumer utilizes material possessions as a proxy measure for success and happiness. In effect materialistic purchases provide only temporary happiness and loneliness prevails. Any attempt to fill this void of lack of happiness through indulgence in more materialistic consumption remains unsuccessful because the consumer has already disturbed the social network and has lower prospects of social sharing, resulting in greater loneliness. An unhappy consumer indulges in more materialism to shake off these feelings, resulting in greater loneliness, which leads to more unhappiness. The unhappiness from materialistic purchases results in continuous brand/product switching, undesirable post-purchase evaluations and shifting brand loyalties, which is a concern for theorists and marketers alike.

The trap has been established theoretically, in less exhaustive forms, previously. However, concrete efforts to provide a theoretical understanding of how the consumer can break free of the trap have yet not transpired from the prior discussion. The existing research remains inadequate in furnishing contingencies that can make the phenomenon directly researchable. Furthermore, materialism has been widely discussed and researched but a unified materialism theory in relation to consumer happiness has not yet crystallized. It remains fragmented under different disciplines and subjects that study the consumer's life from various social, psychological, cultural and media communicational standpoints.

This book provides an elaborative framework of the predictors, outcomes, consumer reactions and mechanisms of materialism in relation to consumer happiness and establishes a unified Socio-Psychological Theory of the Materialism Trap. The unified theory builds collectively upon the personal, social and psychological factors of the consumer that were previously studied within different subject areas. Furthermore, the study establishes the role of three facets of materialism for channelizing the consumption process such that the consumer can consciously break free from the trap and move towards sustained happiness. It also discovers the contingencies that can further change the materialism-loneliness and loneliness-happiness relationships.

The eight constructs pertaining to the personal–psychological, social, socio-cultural and socio-psychological domains of consumer behaviour are identified as directly impacting the routine of the consumer. Among these, the purchase mechanism, i.e. egocentric and socio-centric motivations, experiential purchases and non-self-engrossing product evaluations, reflects psychological personal motivations; social support reflects the social setup of the consumer; religiosity, social giving and environmentalism reveal socio-cultural identities and nostalgia represents the socio-psychological processes of the consumer.

The theory identified three distinct phases in which the materialism trap can be untangled. The first method is to curb the materialism itself. The second is to weaken the materialism-loneliness relationship and the third is for the consumer to indulge in consumer activities that enhance happiness while weakening the relationship with loneliness.

The first phase of the curbing of materialism starts with the purchase mechanism. It takes into account three main areas where conscious effort by the consumer can help to control it. The consumer's reflection upon extrinsic and intrinsic goal motivations can help differentiate between ego-centric and socio-centric motivations. Thereby, the consumer can plan the purchases beforehand and strike a balance between the two. A good blend of both types of purchases can help the consumer realize both extrinsic and intrinsic goal motivations, while avoiding the stress of the superficial call to dematerialize. In other words, planned decision-making can be more useful to the consumer as it helps in determining and utilizing available resources; determining the exact need for the product, the estimated life and the usage pattern of the product; and the disposal options, thus moving away from materialism. Moreover, during the purchase, an emphasis upon experiential purchases rather than materialistic purchases can provide the consumer with delight, satisfaction, psychological nourishment and cherished moments that can go a long way. Following the purchasing stage is the evaluation stage, which is often when dissatisfaction and unhappiness creeps in. A detachment from the symbolic meaning of the purchase and evaluation on a utilitarian basis can help the consumer to effectively identify and differentiate between what is needed and what is desired.

Social giving can help in reducing materialism as it is a medium that consumers can use to channel their materialistic pursuits. This is because by giving away a portion of disposable income, there remains a lower chance of materialistic expenditure of the remaining income. Moreover, emphasizing the needs of the community and becoming a helping anchor in bringing about change in the lives of others is a major motivation that can shape consumer behaviour. Environmentalism can also be a strong guiding principle for conscious consumers. It motivates towards letting go of materialistic values and shifting away from wasteful consumption patterns. It actively encourages the consumer to indulge in environmentally friendly and sustainable consumption. It is a motivational booster that reduces the materialistic drive while bringing consumers closer to those who have similar beliefs. Finally, religiosity provides a sense of purpose and achievement to the consumer. It not only acts as a guiding principle in daily lives but also motivates towards letting go of materialistic values and exerting control over desires. The religious belief system can help to realign consumption patterns such that they are directed towards helping others and to preserve the milieu with the needed faith and conviction, thus lowering materialism.

The most important factor in weakening the materialism-loneliness relationship is social support. It largely impacts the setup in which the consumer resides. It helps to reduce the anxieties and general insecurities of the consumer, which are the forerunner of materialism, and to reduce loneliness through the availability of more interaction opportunities and enhanced prospects for sharing. Secondly, nostalgia serves as a repository of affection, widens social connectedness and augments the self-worth of the consumer. It is in opposition to materialistic values that focus only on present desires and therefore can counter them through powerful memories of past experiences and people, which are cherished more by the consumer. It highlights personal preciousness for the consumer, which subdues the prestige and status factors attached to the product. In effect, when people feel nostalgic the desire for social connectedness rises, which offsets the desire for money. It also reduces the desire to have, hold onto and obtain prized valuables. Moreover, nostalgia reduces loneliness by acting as a stimulus towards social connectivity, as the consumer exhibits the desire to relive the cherished memories and reconnect to people. It instils social connectedness, increases pro-social behaviour and decreases anti-social behaviour, thereby weakening the relationship between materialism and loneliness. Thirdly, social giving signifies self-transcendence values, which are in opposition to materialistic values. Involvement in such activities can help bring people closer through greater interaction and mutual empathetic appreciation that bridge the isolation and loneliness created by materialism. Finally, environmentalism and religiosity together build up a characteristic value orientation of self-transcendence that helps the consumer to tone down materialism and enhances sharing prospects. They emphasize collective order and community service, instilling a sense of care for the environment and the people around, weakening the link between materialism and loneliness.

The third phase also starts with bringing about a change in the purchase mechanism. Socio-centric purchase motivations provide more awareness and connectivity, whereas experiential purchases provide soulful nourishment and satisfaction. Those that are more engaging and intrinsic have a higher capability for furnishing sustained happiness. Next to the purchase stage, it is most often at evaluation stage that dissatisfaction and unhappiness creep in. A detachment from the symbolic meaning of the purchase and evaluation on a utilitarian basis can help the consumer to effectively identify, differentiate and enhance satisfaction and happiness. Social giving can also provide internal satisfaction and soulful nourishment leading to sustained happiness through attending to the needs of others. Moreover, environmentalism instils a sense of purpose, care and accomplishment that fulfils higher-order needs and can play its characteristic role in sustained happiness and enhanced connectivity with the community of like-minded consumers. Similarly, religiosity provides the consumer with a greater level of connectivity with surroundings and people through conservation of the system. It also provides the consumer with a sense of spiritual accomplishment that fulfils higher-order needs. The satisfaction attached to taking care of the community, fulfilling duties and playing a role in system preservation enhances happiness and sustains it at a greater level. Nostalgia also plays an important role in revitalizing the positive affect of the consumer. The consumer feels relaxed and comfortable in remembering good times from the past, which results in enhanced happiness. Finally, social support lessens the feeling of isolation and enhances prospects for sharing, which help to bridge the gap between loneliness and happiness.

The study provides a unified theory for increasing the happiness of consumers who are materialistic and lonely and are stuck in the trap. The conceptualization, relationships and identified contingencies are built upon various theories of materialism. Since materialism is an outgrowth of a combination of unmet higher-order psychological needs, incomplete dubious development of self-concept, and inability to form loving and close social relationships, these perspectives are elucidated by the *motivational theory*. Consumers often try to conciliate unfulfilled core needs with material possessions, yet these are often meaningless substitutes, and are poorer motivations towards well-being. The consumer is thus unable to reach the end goal of happiness. Moreover, the *attachment theory* explains the entrap-ment of the materialistic consumer in loneliness, i.e. whenever basic needs of intimacy and connectivity (primary attachment) are not fulfilled, there is a natural tendency to resort to compensations or substitutes based on mate-rial possessions (secondary attachments). Furthermore, according to the *self-determination theory*, consumers sometimes do not develop a mate-rial lifestyle for reasons of self-esteem or self-portrayal, but rather attach themselves to material possessions either to reflect success or in pursuit of happiness, actually trying to avoid the pain of social isolation. Instead, they make themselves more lonely. Also, as suggested by the *attitude function theory*, such focus on materialistic purchases plays the ego-defensive func-tion for the consumer, making them feel safe, secure and esteemed. However, it disturbs the connectivity of the consumer with others and the consumer becomes lonelier as they indulge more in materialism. Moreover, in rela-tion to acquisition centrality, the *social comparison theory* suggests that as consumers compare and contrast their social and material standing with others on a continuous basis, luxury consumption based on social activities may bring happiness. Consumers can utilize such activities to enhance their appeal, make them more 'wanted' and make them fit in with others, across a myriad of situations. But these effects are only temporary. The comparisons often turn destructive if based solely on materialistic purchases. However, experiential purchases allow such comparisons to be evaluated positively. On the other hand, the *terror management theory* suggests that materialistic consumers experience bad times to a greater extent than do less materialistic consumers, as materialism worsens feelings of stress and anxiety in times of trouble. Such consumers become involved in extensive impulsive buying and conspicuous consumption whenever faced with difficult or threatening situations occurring with high levels of stress and anxiety.

All these theoretical perspectives on materialism indicate it to be a value orientation that is detrimental to consumer happiness over a period of time and one that needs the consumer's attention. The Socio-Psychological Theory of the Materialism Trap answers this call by identifying small yet incremental consumer behaviours that can prevent the consumer being trapped in the cycle of materialism-loneliness-unhappiness. The theory fulfils the promise to iden-tify practical steps for the consumer to untangle the trap in a sustained way.

7.2. Contributions and implications

The study makes a significant theoretical contribution by investigating and theorizing the materialism-loneliness-happiness trap and its impact on the consumer. It provides a systematic review of the materialism literature and introduces a theoretical framework on consumption patterns and subsequent consumer behaviour that will supplement materialism research. The framework advances the academic understanding of the phenomena involved by providing a cross-over underpinning for the combined psychological, personal and social factors surrounding the consumer.

The study contributes to the discipline of *consumer behaviour* as it takes into account the different aspects of the consumption process and the motivations behind it. The study can effectively contribute towards the understanding of the decision-making process at a finer level as it focuses on the consumer decision-making process as a complete purchase mechanism applied at different stages of consumption. The study effectively establishes that materialism can be curbed and manipulated through changes in consumption behaviour and daily routine rather than the impractical call for the dematerializing of the whole lifestyle, which earlier research emphasized. Sustainability of happiness comes with conscious efforts to shape consumption behaviour responsibly and ethically and to make it wholesome. Purchasing and consumption should be aligned in a way that maximizes the pay-offs to the consumer as an individual and benefits those around them.

The conceptual clarity of materialism and related processes presented will at a practical level enable consumers to effectively enlarge their consumption experience and enjoy a higher level of satisfaction with their purchases and experiences. Moreover it will help consumers to relish a sustained level of happiness as *better consumers*, *users* and *givers* within society.

The study can also contribute to the discipline of *brand management*. It is observed that consumers often exhibit post-purchase discontent and unhappiness with the purchases they make, resulting in continuous product and brand switching. Practitioners can help to train consumers through marketing, events, promotions and loyalty programmes to adopt certain consumption patterns that make them happier with their purchases and promote loyalty over a longer period of time.

In addition, the study can contribute to the discipline of *advertising* as it provides theoretical foundations steering practising marketers to use advertising appeals that modify and promote happier consumption patterns. Marketers can effectively reduce the level of product dissatisfaction and brand switching by educating the consumer regarding evaluation-process potholes. Advertising appeals can be streamlined according to the *experiential* and *nostalgic* aspects of products and services. These two areas of appeal can be used in advertising and promotions, increasing not only the chances of higher sales but also the chances of happier consumers. Moreover the study will help marketers to develop marketing campaigns that are more meaningful, environmentally responsible, closer/nostalgic to/ for the consumer and related others, and provide satisfaction by fulfilling the promises made in marketing messages. Marketers can make their promises more eloquent by focusing on social connectivity rather than personal gratification.

7.3 Limitations and directions

The study is conceptual and theoretical in nature and is systematically developed based upon existing literature. The empirical evidence is yet to be provided. All aspects of the theory have to be verified building upon testable hypotheses. The propositions are based on theories from various disciplines relating to the predispositions and impacts of materialism. The theory, however, focuses only on the materialism trap and does not probe the causes of the aforementioned *dispositions of materialism*. The Socio-Psychological Theory of the MLH Trap focuses on the conscious efforts of the individual consumer to break free from the materialism trap for sustained happiness. It does not take into account *macro social aspects* related to materialism such as media campaigns, advertising, public policy implications and political campaigns and how these can contribute towards weakening of the trap. Further elaboration on these aspects may also contribute towards a deeper understanding of the mechanism. Moreover the theory predicts the impacts of materialistic values on the consumer's social, cultural and psychological lifestyle largely at *individual level*. There is a need for future research to investigate the far-reaching impacts of the materialism trap on *interpersonal relationships*, *group dynamics* and *communal behaviour*.

The theory is not an all-inclusive or exhaustive anticipation of the constructs affecting materialism. Rather it focuses only on constructs that are contingencies to the materialism-loneliness-happiness trap. There may be other variables related to antecedents or outcomes of materialism that are not discussed in the study, as the *scope is limited to the materialism trap*.

Social support is a socio-cultural factor that can play a major role in the weakening of the materialism trap. As the theory is built upon existing literature that comes largely from Western culture there is an inherent *systematic bias*. Since materialism exhibits large variations across different societies and nations, future research on cross-cultural comparisons may offer valuable insights on the theory's *ability to moderate* the relationships between materialism, loneliness and happiness across different societies. Moreover, materialism may or may not be affected by varying levels of social support, indicating that materialism is a stronger reality that shapes societal realities and values.

Neither does the theory take into account the *demographic factors* of consumers, which may have profound impact on materialism itself. Future research may focus on this or use it as a control variable, or involve separate studies largely focused on demographic factors alone.

The developed theory is largely correlational and does not offer any anticipatory account of *temporal changes in materialism* over the consumer's life course. This opens up room for both longitudinal and experimental research that may help in establishing causal flows between the pivotal variables and the impact of changes over time. Experimental research may also help in understanding why materialists continue to be dissatisfied with the different aspects of their lives and whether materialism is a cause of lower happiness or vice versa, or whether a bidirectional relationship exists between the two. Longitudinal or multi-wave longitudinal research can play a role in exploring possible mediating mechanisms. This also points towards the need for future research based on triangulation methods.

Moreover, future research may also attempt to conduct cluster analysis and carry out *segmentation of materialists* into segments based on life expectations, life satisfaction, social conditions, evaluation of standard of living based on ideal versus capability standards, and situational prompts.

7.4 Conclusion

Materialism has become established as a strong, prevailing reality of consumerism and has advanced insolently around the world. It has given rise to iniquities such as loneliness and unhappiness that trap the consumer indefinitely. The understanding of this trap and the devising of a solution for consumers to untangle it is becoming significant for both theorists and marketers. The theory that we have developed identifies that in order to save the consumers from the MLH trap the foremost step is to reduce materialism. Secondly, it is also important to mitigate the materialism-loneliness/loneliness-happiness relationship and enhance the prospects of happiness. Thirdly, efforts have to be sustained for a longer period of time. The study establishes a unified theory of the materialism trap and the ways in which it can be untangled in a well-managed and sustained way.

The solution to the materialism-loneliness-happiness trap lies in multipronged social, cultural and psychological interventions that can untangle it. This theory identifies constructs from the social and psychological setup of the consumer that can help reduce materialism, weaken the materialism-loneliness relationship and enhance the level of sustained happiness. Thus can the consumer be helped to *defeat* the materialism trap.

The primary and the most significant role in confronting this trap is to be played by the consumer themselves. It is the consumer's conscious effort that can restrain them from wasteful and unnecessary consumption, increase the purchase of more environmentally friendly products that will last longer, and invest more in experiences and communal goods. Secondly, higher levels of charity, faith and discipline in consumption can enhance sharing prospects and the internal happiness of the consumer. The third role is played by nostalgia and religiosity, which help the consumer to cherish the little onsets of happiness in their life over a longer period of time, be thankful for blessings received and share them with the less fortunate. All these factors together enhance and strengthen sharing prospects and social support of the consumer, which in turn fights the loneliness syndrome experienced by the consumer.

In a nutshell, just as the MLH trap is cyclical and multipronged, the solution to it is also multi-tiered and starts with the realization that better, healthier and more social lifestyles are required to create better consumers who can really cherish their consumption experiences. Similarly, advertisers and marketers can develop longer-lasting bonds and stronger brand equity by focusing on experience-based social marketing.

Appendices

7.1A Coding categorization for constructs and journals

Materialism	M	*American Psychologist*	1	AP
Happiness	H	*Journal of Applied Social Psychology*	2	JASP
Loneliness	L	*Journal of Consumer Policy*	3	JCP
Materialism and well-being	MWB	*Journal of Consumer Psychology*	4	JCPsy
Materialism and happiness	MH	*Journal of Consumer Research*	5	JCR
Materialism and loneliness	ML	*Journal of Happiness Studies*	6	JHS
Materialism and green consumption	MGC	*Journal of Marketing Research*	7	JMR
Materialism and social support	MSS	*Journal of Personality and Social Psychology*	8	JPSP
Materialism-loneliness-happiness	MLH	*Journal of the Academy of Marketing Science*	9	JAMS
Loneliness and happiness	LH	*Personality and Individual Differences*	10	PID
Social support	SS	*Psychological Inquiry*	11	PI
Social support and loneliness	SSL	*Psychology & Marketing*	12	P&M
Social support and happiness	SSH	*Social Indicators Research*	13	SIR
		Journal of Social Psychology	14	JSP
		Human Relations	15	HR
		North American Journal of Psychology	16	NAJP
		Advances in Consumer Research	17	ACR
		Journal of Economic Psychology	18	JEP
		Harvard Business Review	19	HBR
		Others	20	O

7.1B Presence of key constructs in selected journals

Key words	AP	JASP	JCP	JCPsy	JCR	JHS	JMR	JPSP	JAMS	PID	PI	P&M	SIR	JSP	Total	%
Materialism	13	16	19	61	65	106	115	21	95	147	98	31	313	17	1170	
M & well-being	4	4	0	4	14	20	13	1	38	61	35	15	107	1	317	27.1
M & happiness	3	5	16	11	10	32	30	3	15	21	22	7	78	8	261	22.3
M & loneliness	1	1	1	1	2	4	2	1	0	9	4	4	11	1	42	3.6
M & green consumption	0	5	0	16	5	4	7	11	8	3	5	5	19	3	91	7.8
M & social support	5	1	2	29	34	43	62	5	34	53	30	0	94	57	449	38.4
M-L-H	0	0	0	0	0	3	1	0	0	0	2	0	4	0	10	0.9

M=Materialism, L=Loneliness, H=Happiness

Retrieved May 2015

7.1C Most frequently recurring authors and their contribution to various areas of materialism literature

Serial No.	Authors	Research Area
1	Deci, E. L.	Happiness potentials/materialism
2	Ryan, R. M.	Happiness potentials/materialism
3	Dawson, S.	Materialism scales and values orientation
4	Richins, M. L.	Materialism scales and values orientation/ happiness potentials
5	Seligman, M. E.	Materialism and well-being
6	Williams, R.	Problems of materialism/cross-cultural materialism
7	Kasser, T.	Problems of materialism/materialism and well-being
8	Belk, R. W.	Materialism scales and values orientation
9	Argyle, M.	Materialism and well-being
10	Rindfleisch, A.	Happiness potentials/materialism/consumption
11	Burroughs, J. E.	Happiness potentials/materialism/consumption
12	Diener, E.	Materialism and happiness
13	Shwartz, S. H.	Cross-cultural materialism and happiness
14	Gilovich, T.	Materialism and its impacts
15	VanBoven, L.	Materialism and its impacts/materialism and happiness
16	Kaplan, S.	Consumption/materialism and well-being
17	Ahuvia, A. C.	Materialism and well-being
18	Sirgy, M. J.	Materialism and its impacts
19	Haller, M.	Cross-cultural happiness and materialism
20	Arkin, R. M.	Materialism and its impacts/uncertainty
21	Sethia, N.	Sustainable consumption
22	Kotler, P.	Reinventing marketing
23	Watson, J. J.	Consumption/materialism
24	Muncy, J. A.	Consumer ethics and materialism
25	Wong, N. Y.	Value-based materialism
26	Holt, D. B.	Consumption/materialism and well-being
27	Dittmar, H.	Consumption/materialism and well-being

(continued)

Serial No.	Authors	Research Area
28	Carter, T. J.	Consumption/materialism
29	Eastman, J. K.	Consumer ethics and materialism
30	Roberts, J. A.	Materialism and its impacts/materialism and happiness
31	Clement, A.	Materialism and its impacts/materialism and happiness
32	Hsee, C. K.	Consumption/materialism
33	Hadler, M.	Cross-cultural happiness and materialism
34	Hudders, L.	Consumption/materialism
35	Pandelaere, M.	Consumption/materialism
36	Chang, L.	Materialism and its impacts/uncertainty
37	Twitchell, J. B.	Materialism

7.1D Prominent authors on materialism and their frequently cited articles

Author (s)	Year	Title	Journal	Cited by	Code
Deci, E. L. and Ryan, R. M.	2000	The "what" and "why" of goal pursuits: Human needs and the self-determination of behavior	*Harvard Business Review*	9683	19-H
Ryan, R. M. and Deci, E. L.	2001	On happiness and human potentials: A review of research on hedonic and eudemonic well-being	*Annual Review of Psychology*	3729	20-H
Zimet, G. D., Dahlem, N. W., Zimet, S. G., and Farley, G. K.	1988	The multidimensional scale of perceived social support	*Journal of Personality Assessment*	3075	20-SS
Schwartz, S. H.	1999	A theory of cultural values and some implications for work	*Applied Psychology*	2049	20-H
Cohen, S. and Hoberman, H. M.	1983	Positive events and social supports as buffers of life change stress	*Journal of Applied Social Psychology*	1962	2-SS
Richins, M. L. and Dawson, S.	1992	A consumer values orientation for materialism and its measurement: Scale development and validation	*Journal of Consumer Research*	1814	5-M
Diener, E. and Seligman, M. E.	2004	Beyond money: Toward an economy of well-being	*Psychological Science in the Public Interest*	1575	20-MWB
Williams, R.	1996	Problems of materialism	*Design and Aesthetics: A Reader*	1485	20-M
Holt, D. B.	1995	How consumers consume: A typology of consumption practices	*Journal of Consumer Research*	1419	5-M
Belk, R. W.	1985	Materialism: Trait aspects of living in the material world	*Journal of Consumer Research*	1403	5-M

(continued)

7.1D continued

Author (s)	Year	Title	Journal	Cited by	Code
Tatzel, M.	2003	The art of buying: Coming to terms with money and materialism	*Journal of Happiness Studies*	1074	6-M
Argyle, M.	2003	18 causes and correlates of happiness	*Well-Being: The Foundations of Hedonic Psychology*	1058	20-M
Diener, E., Lucas, R. E., and Scollon, C. N.	2006	Beyond the hedonic treadmill: Revising the adaptation theory of well-being	*American Psychologist*	942	1-MWB
Richins, M. L.	1994	Valuing things: The public and private meanings of possessions	*Journal of Consumer Research*	873	5-M
Richins, M. L.	1994	Special possessions and the expression of material values	*Journal of Consumer Research*	717	5-M
Burroughs, J. E., and Rindfleisch, A.	2002	Materialism and well-being: A conflicting values perspective	*Journal of Consumer Research*	679	5-WB
Diener, E. and Oishi, S.	2000	Money and happiness: Income and subjective well-being across nations	*Culture and Subjective Well-Being*	598	20-MH
Belk, R. W.	1984	Three scales to measure constructs related to materialism: Reliability, validity, and relationships to measures of happiness	*Advances in Consumer Research*	567	17-M
Kasser, T. and Ryan, R. M.	2001	Be careful what you wish for: Optimal functioning and the relative attainment of intrinsic and extrinsic goals	*Towards a Positive Psychology of Human Striving*	437	20-M
Csikszentmihalyi, M. and Hunter, J.	2003	Happiness in everyday life: The uses of experience sampling	*Journal of Happiness Studies*	421	6-H
Ger, G. and Belk, R. W.	1996	Cross-cultural differences in materialism	*Journal of Economic Psychology*	396	18-M

Rindfleisch, A., Burroughs, J. E., and Denton, F.	1997	Family structure, materialism, and compulsive consumption	Journal of Consumer Research	391	5-MWB
Van Boven, L. and Gilovich, T.	2003	To do or to have? That is the question	Journal of Personality and Social Psychology	385	8-M
Hills, P. and Argyle, M.	2002	The Oxford Happiness Questionnaire: A compact scale for the measurement of psychological well-being	Personality and individual differences	369	10-H
Kaplan, S.	2000	New ways to promote pro-environmental behaviour: Human nature and environmentally responsible behaviour	Journal of Social Issues	367	20-MGC
Kasser, T. and Ahuvia, A.	2002	Materialistic values and well-being in business students	European Journal of Social Psychology	324	20-MWB
Hawkley, L. C. and Cacioppo, J. T.	2010	Loneliness matters: A theoretical and empirical review of consequences and mechanisms	Annals of Behavioural Medicine	322	20-L
Belk, R.	2010	Sharing	Journal of Consumer Research	302	5-SS
Sirgy, M. J.	1998	Materialism and quality of life	Social Indicators Research	295	13-M
Haller, M. and Hadler, M.	2006	How social relations and structures can produce happiness and unhappiness: An international comparative analysis	Social Indicators Research	273	13-SS
Richins, M. L.	1987	Media, materialism, and human happiness	Advances in Consumer Research	269	17-MH
Chang, L. and Arkin, R. M.	2002	Materialism as an attempt to cope with uncertainty	Psychology and Marketing	215	12-M

(continued)

7.1D continued

Author (s)	Year	Title	Journal	Cited by	Code
Dittmar, H.	2005	Compulsive buying—a growing concern? An examination of gender, age, and endorsement of materialistic values as predictors	*British Journal of Psychology*	214	20-M
Bauer, M. A., Wilkie, J. E., Kim, J. K., and Bodenhausen, G. V.	2012	Cuing consumerism: Situational materialism undermines personal and social well-being	*Psychological Science*	211	20-MWB
Sheth, J. N., Sethia, N. K., and Srinivas, S.	2011	Mindful consumption: A customer-centric approach to sustainability	*Journal of the Academy of Marketing Science*	210	9-MGC
Rook, K. S.	1984	Promoting social bonding: Strategies for helping the lonely and socially isolated	*American Psychologist*	208	1-SSL
Weiss, R. S.	1987	Reflections on the present state of loneliness research	*Journal of Social Behaviour and Personality*	200	20-L
Kotler, P.	2011	Reinventing marketing to manage the environmental imperative	*Journal of Marketing*	190	20-MGC
La Barbera, P. A. and Gürhan, Z.	1997	The role of materialism, religiosity, and demographics in subjective well-being	*Psychology and Marketing*	188	12-MWB
Goldberg, M. E., Gorn, G. J., Peracchio, L. A., and Bamossy, G.	2003	Understanding materialism among youth	*Journal of Consumer Psychology*	182	4-M
Thogersen, J. and Crompton, T.	2009	Simple and painless? The limitations of spillover in environmental campaigning	*Journal of Consumer Policy*	169	3-MGC

Author	Year	Title	Journal		
Fave, D. A., Brdar, I., Freire, T., Vella-Brodrick, D., and Wissing, M. P.	2011	The eudemonic and hedonic components of happiness: Qualitative and quantitative findings	Social Indicators Research	162	13-H
Van Boven, L.	2005	Experientialism, materialism, and the pursuit of happiness	Review of General Psychology	158	20-MH
Rindfleisch, A., Burroughs, J. E., and Wong, N.	2009	The safety of objects: Materialism, existential insecurity, and brand connection	Journal of Consumer Research	153	5-M
Watson, J. J.	2003	The relationship of materialism to giving tendencies, saving, and debt	Journal of Economic Psychology	145	18-M
Lu, L.	1999	Personal or environmental causes of happiness: A longitudinal analysis	Journal of Social Psychology	139	14-H
Muncy, J. A. and Eastman, J. K.	1998	Materialism and consumer ethics: An exploratory study	Journal of Business Ethics	135	20-M
Kilbourne, W. and Pickett, G.	2008	How materialism affects environmental beliefs, concern, and environmentally responsible behavior	Journal of Business Research	134	20-MGC
Ahuvia, A. C. and Wong, N. Y.	2002	Personality and values based materialism: Their relationship and origins	Journal of Consumer Psychology	132	4-M
Hudders, L. and Pandelaere, M.	2012	The silver lining of materialism: The impact of luxury consumption on subjective well-being	Journal of Happiness Studies	131	6-MWB
Chancellor, J. and Lyubomirsky, S.	2011	Happiness and thrift: When (giving) less is (hedonically) more	Journal of Consumer Psychology	131	4-MH
Dunn, E. W., Gilbert, D. T., and Wilson, T. D.	2011	If money doesn't make you happy, then you probably aren't spending it right	Journal of Consumer Psychology	131	4-MH
Kasser, T., Rosenblum, K. L., Sameroff, A. J., Deci, E. L., Niemiec, C. P., Ryan, R. M., and Hawks, S.	2014	Changes in materialism, changes in psychological well-being: Evidence from three longitudinal studies and an intervention experiment	Motivation and Emotion	124	20-MWB

(continued)

7.1D continued

Author (s)	Year	Title	Journal	Cited by	Code
Mellor, D., Stokes, M., Firth, L., Hayashi, Y., and Cummins, R.	2008	Need for belonging, relationship satisfaction, loneliness, and life satisfaction	*Personality and Individual Differences*	121	10-SSL
Carter, T. J. and Gilovich, T.	2010	The relative relativity of material and experiential purchases	*Journal of Personality and Social Psychology*	116	8-MH
Flouri, E.	1999	An integrated model of consumer materialism: Can economic socialization and maternal values predict materialistic attitudes in adolescents?	*Journal of Socio-Economics*	112	20-M
Soscia, I.	2007	Gratitude, delight, or guilt: The role of consumers' emotions in predicting post-consumption behaviours	*Psychology and Marketing*	107	12-MH
Nicolao, L., Irwin, J. R., and Goodman, J. K.	2009	Happiness for sale: Do experiential purchases make consumers happier than material purchases?	*Journal of Consumer Research*	106	5-MH
Ger, G. and Belk, R. W.	1999	Accounting for materialism in four cultures	*Journal of Material Culture*	104	20-M
Pepper, M., Jackson, T., and Uzzell, D.	2009	An examination of the values that motivate socially conscious and frugal consumer behaviours	*International Journal of Consumer Studies*	103	20-MGC
Flatters, P. and Willmott, M.	2009	Understanding the post-recession consumer	*Harvard Business Review*	102	19-M
Kilbourne, W., Grünhagen, M., and Foley, J.	2005	A cross-cultural examination of the relationship between materialism and individual values	*Journal of Economic Psychology*	100	18-M

7.1E Other most-related journal articles over the last 15 years

Authors	Year	Title	Journal	Cited by	Code
Roberts, J. A. and Clement, A.	2007	Materialism and satisfaction with over-all quality of life and eight life domains	Social Indicators Research	95	13-M
Hsee, C. K., Yang, Y., Li, N., and Shen, L.	2009	Wealth, warmth, and well-being: Whether happiness is relative or absolute depends on whether it is about money, acquisition, or consumption	Journal of Marketing Research	93	7-MH
Ahuvia, A.	2008	If money doesn't make us happy, why do we act as if it does?	Journal of Economic Psychology	92	18-MH
Hurst, M., Dittmar, H., Bond, R., and Kasser, T.	2013	The relationship between materialistic values and environmental attitudes and behaviours: A meta-analysis	Journal of Environmental Psychology	87	20-MGC
Yoon, S. and Vargas, P. T.	2006	On the psychology of materialism: Wanting things, having things, and being happy	Advertising and Society	75	20-MH
Huang, M. H. and Rust, R. T.	2011	Sustainability and consumption	Journal of the Academy of Marketing Science	75	9-MGC
Wildschut, T., Sedikides, C., Routledge, C., Arndt, J., and Cordaro, R.	2010	Nostalgia as a repository of social connectedness: The role of attachment-related avoidance	Journal of Personality and Social Psychology	74	8-MSS
Diener, E. and Biswas-Diener, R.	2002	Will money increase subjective well-being?	Social Indicators Research	71	13-MWB

(continued)

7.1E continued

Authors	Year	Title	Journal	Cited by	Code
Ahuvia, A. C. and Wong, N.	1999	Materialism: Origins and implications for personal well-being	European Advances in Consumer Research	71	20-MWB
Zhou, X. and Gao, D. G.	2008	Social support and money as pain management mechanisms	Psychological Inquiry	68	11-MSS
McDonald, S., Oates, C., Thyne, M., Alevizou, P., and McMorland, L. A.	2009	Comparing sustainable consumption patterns across product sectors	International Journal of Consumer Studies	67	20-MGC
Ryan, L. and Dziurawiec, S.	2001	Materialism and its relationship to life satisfaction	Social Indicators Research	55	13-MH
Howell, R. T. and Hill, G.	2009	The mediators of experiential purchases: Determining the impact of psychological needs satisfaction and social comparison	Journal of Positive Psychology	49	20-M
Wang, J. and Wallendorf, M.	2006	Materialism, status signaling, and product satisfaction	Journal of the Academy of Marketing Science	48	9-MH
Christopher, A. N., Kuo, S. V., Abraham, K. M., Noel, L. W., and Linz, H. E.	2004	Materialism and affective well-being: The role of social support	Personality and Individual Differences	47	10-MWB
DeLeire, T. and Kalil, A.	2010	Does consumption buy happiness? Evidence from the United States	International Review of Economics	46	20-MH
Kasser, T.	2006	Materialism and its alternatives	Journal of Consumer Research	45	5-M

Author	Year	Title	Journal		
Deckop, J. R., Jurkiewicz, C. L., and Giacalone, R. A.	2010	Effects of materialism on work-related personal well-being	Human Relations	45	15-MWB
Podoshen, J. S. and Andrzejewski, S. A.	2012	An examination of the relationships between materialism, conspicuous consumption, impulse buying, and brand loyalty	Journal of Marketing Theory and Practice	40	20-M
Ginter, E., Glauser, A., and Richmond, B. O.	1999	Loneliness, social support, and anxiety among two South Pacific cultures	Psychological Reports	36	20-SSL
Kurtz, J. L., Wilson, T. D., and Gilbert, D. T.	2007	Quantity versus uncertainty: When winning one prize is better than winning two	Journal of Experimental Social Psychology	32	20-ML
Royo, M.	2008	Consumption and subjective wellbeing: Exploring basic needs, social comparison, social integration and hedonism in Peru	Social Indicators Research	27	13-MH
Mauss, I. B, Savino, N. S., Anderson, C. L., Weisbuch, M., Tamir, M., and Laudenslager, M. L.	2012	The pursuit of happiness can be lonely	Emotion	27	20-LH
Park, J. K. and Deborah. R. J.	2011	More than meets the eye: The influence of implicit and explicit self-esteem on materialism	Journal of Consumer Psychology	27	4-MH
Sirgy, M. J., Gurel-Atay, E., Webb, D., Cicic, M., Husic-Mehmedovic, M., Ekici, A., . . . and Johar, J. S.	2013	Is materialism all that bad? Effects on satisfaction with material life, life satisfaction, and economic motivation	Social Indicators Research	26	13-MH

(continued)

7.1E continued

Authors	Year	Title	Journal	Cited by	Code
Ang, C. S., Mansor, A. T., and Tan, K. A.	2014	Pangs of loneliness breed material lifestyle but don't power up life satisfaction of young people: The moderating effect of gender	Social indicators Research	26	13-ML
Weinberger, M. F. and Wallendorf, M.	2008	Having vs. doing: Materialism, experientialism, and the experience of materiality	Advances in Consumer Research	25	17-MLH
Luna, D. and Forquer Gupta, S.	2001	An integrative framework for cross-cultural consumer behavior	International Marketing Review	21	20-MH
Ahuvia, A. C. and Wong, N. Y.	2002	Personality and values based materialism: Their relationship and origins	Journal of Consumer Psychology	20	4-M
Pieters, R.	2013	Bidirectional dynamics of materialism and loneliness: Not just a vicious cycle	Journal of Consumer Research	20	5-ML
Goldsmith, R. E. and Clark, R. A.	2012	Materialism, status consumption, and consumer independence	Journal of Social Psychology	18	14-ML
Rindfleisch, A. and Burroughs, J. E.	2004	Terrifying thoughts, terrible materialism? Contemplations on a terror management account of materialism and consumer behavior	Journal of Consumer Psychology	17	4-M

Promislo, M. D., Deckop, J. R., Giacalone, R. A., and Jurkiewicz, C. L.	2010	Valuing money more than people: The effects of materialism on work–family conflict	*Journal of Occupational and Organisational Psychology*	14	20-ML
Hombrados-Mendieta, I., García-Martín, M. A., and Gómez-Jacinto, L.	2013	The relationship between social support, loneliness, and subjective well-being in a Spanish sample from a multidimensional perspective	*Social Indicators Research*	11	13-SSL
Clarke III, I. and Micken, K. S.	2002	An exploratory cross-cultural analysis of the values of materialism	*Journal of International Consumer Marketing*	8	20-M
Larsen, V., Sirgy, M. J., and Wright, N. D.	1999	Materialism: The construct, measures, antecedents, and consequences	*Academy of Marketing Studies Journal*	7	20-M
Tsang, J. A., Carpenter, T. P., Roberts, J. A., Frisch, M. B., and Carlisle, R.	2014	Why are materialists less happy? The role of gratitude and need satisfaction in the relationship between materialism and life satisfaction	*Personality and Individual Differences*	7	10-MH
Tilikidou, I. and Delistavrou, A.	2004	The influence of the materialistic values on consumers' pro-environmental post-purchase behavior	*American Marketing Association Winter Educators' Conference*	4	20-MGC

(continued)

Authors	Year	Title	Journal	Cited by	Code
Burroughs, J. E., Chaplin, L. N., Pandelaere, M., Norton, M. I.and Dinauer, L.	2013	Using motivation theory to develop a transformative consumer research agenda for reducing materialism in society	*Journal of Public Policy*	4	20-MLH
Caldas, S. B.	2010	The happiness-to-consumption ratio: An alternative approach in the quest for happiness	*Estudios Gerenciales*	3	20-MH
Scott, K.	2009	Terminal materialism vs. instrumental materialism: Can materialism be beneficial?	*(Doctoral dissertation, Oklahoma State University)*	2	20-MH
Srikant, M.	2013	Materialism in consumer behaviour and marketing: A review	*Management and Marketing, 8(2)*	2	20-M
Mathur, A.	2013	Materialism and charitable giving: Can they co-exist?	*Journal of Consumer Behaviour*	1	20-MSS
Ruvio, A., Somer, E., and Rindfleisch, A.	2014	When bad gets worse: The amplifying effect of materialism on traumatic stress and maladaptive consumption	*Journal of the Academy of Marketing Science*	1	9-ML

7.1F Selected frequently cited books relevant to key constructs

Author(s)	Year	Book Title	Cited By
Schwartz, B.	2004	*The Paradox of Choice: Why More is Less*	2430
Cohen, S., Mermelstein, R., Kamarck, T., and Hoberman, H. M.	1985	*Social Support: Theory, Research and Applications*	1704
Kasser, T.	2003	*The High Price of Materialism*	1481
Lane, R. E.	2000	*The Loss of Happiness in Market Democracies*	1120
Schor, J.	2004	*Born to Buy: The Commercialized Child and the New Consumer Culture*	958
Lin, N., Dean, A., and Ensel, W. M.	2013	*Social Support, Life Events and Depression*	616
Cacioppo, J. T. and Patrick, W.	2008	*Loneliness: Human Nature and the Need for Human Connection*	553
Diener, E. and Biswas-Diener, R.	2008	*Happiness: Unlocking the Mysteries of Psychological Wealth*	522
Williams, R.	2005	*Culture and Materialism: Selected Essays*	321
Young, J. E.	1982	*Loneliness: A Sourcebook of Current theory, Research and Therapy*	260
Twitchell, J. B.	2013	*Lead Us Into Temptation: The Triumph of American Materialism*	249
Tyler, T. R.	2010	*Why People Cooperate: The Role of Social Motivations*	169
Gordon, S.	1976	*Lonely in America*	157
Kardes, F. R., Cronley, M. L., and Cline, T. W.	2010	*Consumer Behaviour: Science and Practice*	93
Guriev, S. M. and Zhuravskaya, E.	2009	*(Un) Happiness in Transition*	78
East, R., Wright, M., and Vanhuele, M.	2013	*Consumer Behaviour: Applications in Marketing*	70
Hammerslough, J.	2009	*Dematerializing: Taming the Power of Possessions*	16
Solomon, M. R, Baboosy, J., Askegaard S. T., and Hogg, M. K.	2013	*Consumer Behaviour: A European Perspective*	3

Index

Page numbers in *italics* refer to information in figures; those in **bold** refer to tables.

Printed in the United States
by Baker & Taylor Publisher Services